MICHAEL BARNES, ROBIN BRIGHTWELL,
ADRIANA VON HAGEN, MARK LEHNER, CYNTHIA PAGE

SECRETS OF LOST
EMPIRES

RECONSTRUCTING THE GLORIES OF AGES PAST

Sterling Publishing Co., Inc.
New York

AUTHORS' ACKNOWLEDGEMENTS

Michael Barnes would like to thank Jan Adkins
for his help in writing *The Obelisk*.
Robin Brightwell would like to thank Tania Lindon
who contributed extensively to *The Colosseum*.
Adriana von Hagen would like to thank Edward Franquemont
for his contribution to *The Incas*.

PICTURE CREDITS

BBC Books would like to thank the following for providing photographs and for permission to reproduce copyright material. While every effort has been made to trace and acknowledge all copyright holders, we would like to apologize should there have been any errors or omissions.

BBC Books pages 32, 34, 35, 42, 43 (Brian Ritchie); 169, 172, 173, 177 (Michelle Chaplow); American Museum of Natural History (J B Taylor), Courtesy Department of Library Services 220; Ancient Art & Architecture Collection 156b, 161; Arcaid 154r (Peter Cook); Michael Barnes 94, 100, 101tl, 108, 112, 124l, 129t, 133b; Index/The Bridgeman Art Library 50; The British Library 116; Copyright British Museum 81; Julian Charrington 165; English Heritage Photographic Library 8, 24 (Skyscan Balloon Photography), 28 (supplied by Wessex Archaeology) 13, 17, 25, 39; Mary Evans Picture Library 154l; Robert Harding Picture Library 180 (Chris Rennie); Hulton Deutsch Collection 119; Christopher Lee 216b; Mark Lehner 53, 54, 55, 57, 59, 62, 63, 67, 71, 75, 78, 79, 84, 87r, 91, 92, 101bl, 101r, 113, 124r, 125, 129b, 132, 133t; Bruce Ludwig 87l; Loren McIntyre 189, 192/3, 192i, 221; Harpers Weekly Feb 12, 1881 (Drawn by F Cozzens), Courtesy of The New York Pubic Library 121; Réunion des Musées Nationaux 117; Scala 144, 156t, 168; Tony Stone Images 46, 136, 140/1, 184i; Adriana von Hagen 184, 201, 205, 208, 213, 216tl, 216r, 218.

This book is published to accompany the television series *Secrets of Lost Empires*, a co-production of BBC and NOVA/WGBH-Boston, first broadcast in 1996.
Executive producers: Michael Barnes (NOVA/WGBH) and Robin Brightwell (BBC)
Producers: Michael Barnes and Cynthia Page
Grateful acknowledgement is made to WGBH Boston for the right to include the chapter 'The Pyramid', which is based on the NOVA program *This Old Pyramid*.
© *Introduction* and *The Colosseum* Robin Brightwell 1996
© *Stonehenge* Cynthia Page 1996 © *The Obelisk* Michael Barnes 1996
© *The Pyramid* Mark Lehner 1996 © *The Incas* Adriana von Hagen 1996

Maps and illustrations by David Brown

Library of Congress Cataloging-in-Publication Available

2   4   6   8   10   9   7   5   3   1

Published 1997 by Sterling Publishing Company, Inc.
387 Park Avenue South, New York, N.Y. 10016
Originally published in Great Britain in 1996 by BBC Books,
an imprint of BBC Worldwide Publishing
Distributed in Canada by Sterling Publishing
% Canadian Manda Group, One Atlantic Avenue, Suite 105
Toronto, Ontario, Canada M6K 3E7
Printed and bound in China
All rights reserved

Sterling ISBN 0-8069-9584-X

CONTENTS

INTRODUCTION

ROBIN BRIGHTWELL

Thousands of years ago great monuments were built by ancient builders who knew only primitive technologies and worked with Stone Age tools. Archaeologists and engineers have speculated at length about how these extraordinary achievements were possible: but, because nobody's theory has been put to the test, the techniques of these builders have remained a mystery. Would it even be feasible for modern humans to use the old tools and to rebuild Stonehenge, the sophisticated architecture of the Roman Empire, the pyramids and obelisks of Ancient Egypt or Sacsawaman, the Incas' city in the clouds? *Secrets of Lost Empires* decided to take on these tasks. It was to be a series of experiments on screen that would pit our modern knowledge of science and engineering against the pragmatic and clearly successful methods of ancient peoples.

We searched for the leading experts, usually archaeologists, who would know which tools and ways of working were used in each of the cultures in question. The experts nearly always had theories about how the monuments were constructed, but once we started to consult more practical people such as stonemasons, builders or engineers, the archaeologists' theories came in for a lot of criticism, based on pure practicality or the laws of mechanics. Clearly, we had to build teams to suit each project.

For some monuments, like the pyramids, the practical skills of a stonemason were enough to set the project going. Others, like Stonehenge, turned out to be far more complicated. The mechanical principles behind the moving, up-ending and accurate siting of a 40-tonne stone turned out to tax even the most sophisticated of today's engineers, computers and all. Perhaps the very complexity of our modern ways of working was preventing us from perceiving these lost techniques. As our stonemason showed, there are sometimes ways of moving giant objects that simply rely upon experience and common sense. We soon came to accept that the ancient builders possessed as least as much of both these commodities as today's craftsmen.

Some of the monuments, like the Colosseum, the great amphitheatre begun by the Emperor Vespasian in Ancient Rome, were built under great pressure of time, the Colosseum itself in no more than eight years. Others, such as Stonehenge, were a more leisurely build: a few hundred years. But in every one of our modern-day projects there was a fixed time for construction, at most a few weeks. This was an added pressure but essential if our films were to keep within their budget. During the months of planning, we had to design a way to build each monument that would be both fast and cheap.

Our engineers were allowed the full range of up-to-date technology at the design and testing stages, but once they actually started to build they would have to show that the old tools worked and were sufficient for the task. For example, engineers were allowed their computers to model and test ways of moving the vast stone blocks up and down the Wiltshire hills on the long journey to the Stonehenge site. But when they set teams of pullers to work and actually tried to move the stones, steel and pulleys were not allowed since neither of these had been invented when Stonehenge was built. Once we had shown that we could carry out a particular task, any repetition of it was done using modern machinery. Otherwise we put a lot of effort into not 'cheating'.

Safety had to be a vital consideration, even if this meant being anachronistic at times: although Stone Age builders did not wear hard hats, or Roman riggers safety harnesses, our workers had to use them. A lesson soon learnt was that all our ancient builders, whether they were Aswani granite craftsmen in Egypt, the Incas, the Ancient Romans or even the Ancient Britons, were as clever as the brightest engineers working for our foremost construction companies today. This surprised us programme-makers, but it also punctured a few engineering egos.

This was impressed upon us when we tried to re-erect the largest group of stones at Stonehenge. The mystery is how a culture using flint tools could shape giant stones weighing up to 40 tonnes, the weight of about five hundred well-built adult men, and move them for miles up hill and down dale without wheels or roads. After that, they up-ended the stones in pits that they had dug in the chalk and lifted 10-tonne lintels on top. These lintel stones had accurate joints in them, and are made of the hardest stone in the British Isles. The most staggering achievement is that, although Stonehenge is built on sloping ground, the lintels are level all the way round. Not only did the ancient builders lift the stones up, but they did it with an accuracy that would make a modern stonemason proud. Our experiments were an attempt to unlock a few of the Ancient Britons' secrets.

There were gifted engineers at work in many ancient civilizations, whose names have never been recorded. Without them there would be no great monuments still standing today. While the Britons were lifting lintels, the Pharaohs of the Old Kingdom were harnessing even more manpower to construct their tombs. The mystery of how they did this was the first to be tackled by us, and led to the idea of the series.

Michael Barnes has always taken risks. I first met him in 1985, when he was making a film on leprosy for the BBC's *Horizon*. Five years later I went to look him up in Boston, and was told that he was in Egypt 'rebuilding a Pyramid'! This sounded as if he had bitten off rather more than even the most ambitious producer should.

The big problem with a pyramid is how you make the sides straight: they have a natural tendency to curve as the structure grows. But Michael's team knew what they were doing and successfully built a small replica of one of the Great Pyramids using full-sized stone blocks and Ancient Egyptian technology. It was the success of this programme, shown in both Britain and the USA in 1994, which inspired us to tackle the secrets of other lost empires.

In order to celebrate their jubilees and honour the sun god the Pharaohs erected the most surprising of their monuments, the obelisk. They are single stones, hewn from solid granite. Their source lies miles up the Nile from the sites where they were erected. On a return visit to Egypt, Michael Barnes and the original pyramids team decided to attempt a task which had often beaten the Egyptians: to quarry, transport and erect their own obelisks. The stone must be quarried without stressing it unevenly, which splits it. If the Egyptians had sometimes failed, as broken obelisks in the granite quarries prove, then what chance for modern amateurs? Even if the obelisk could be got out in one piece, it then had to be manoeuvred on to a barge and finally erected on its pedestal. Michael and his team discovered that their task was very difficult and that they had to consider as many ideas for getting their obelisks upright as they had team members.

If the citizens of Ancient Rome revolted, they could topple the Emperor. To stay in power, the Emperors kept the population satisfied by the most powerful entertainment ever devised: carnage. Tens of thousands of citizens would sit and watch the organized slaughter of animals and human beings, from morning until night. Only one thing was capable of weakening the citizens' enthusiasm and sending them back out on to the streets to plot their master's downfall: the sun. To this day, southern Europe shuts down for several hours at lunchtime. Yet the gory entertainment in the amphitheatres continued despite the intense heat of the midday sun. This was made possible by giant coverings over the banks of seats. These *vela*, or awnings, were as big as the coverings of our modern football and Olympic stadia, yet they were made using the crude materials and technology of two thousand years ago. The secrets of their construction were lost when the Empire collapsed, because none of the methods was recorded and presumably all the materials used to make them have rotted away.

Enthusiasm for these ephemeral, yet highly symbolic structures was whipped up by the researcher on our team, Tania Lindon. She perceived the fascination and challenge of these first-ever giant lightweight roofs. We decided to take on the challenge of building a structure which not only no longer existed, but for which the evidence was at best sketchy and was at worst a confusing series of vague Roman images.

Long after the Romans dominated Europe, an isolated empire developed in what came to be called the New World. The Kingdom of the Incas was as controlled as that of the Romans, but had to achieve that control without the benefit of wheels or horses. As with all systems of social control before or since, the Inca or Emperor needed an efficient communication network. Without it, control cannot be exerted by rulers over distances, and news of the provinces cannot reach the capital.

Instead of horses and wheels the Inca used men. Runners carried messages hundreds of miles from one end of the Empire to the other. They worked in relays, but even so they would have been virtually useless without a method of shortening their journeys.

Peru is a mountainous land but the Incas bridged its gorges, so reducing distances drastically. They built suspension bridges made from grass ropes. The task of re-creating these grass bridges was tackled in a different way from others in *Secrets of Lost Empires* because there are still people in Peru who claim to know how to span mountain gorges with no more than a few home-made ropes. Once Michael Barnes discovered this, he could not resist putting these people's claim to the test.

Peru presented us with a double mystery to solve. Inca structures, whether they are the retaining walls of their bridges and roads or their stunning citadels in the clouds, show an extraordinary ability to handle and shape huge stones. Inca masons trimmed huge boulders and assembled them in smoothly finished walls with near-perfect joints that a knife cannot penetrate. These walls were not only impressive to the eye, but structurally sound. They have successfully withstood frequent earthquakes, while Spanish colonial buildings have tumbled and been repeatedly repaired after each major earthquake.

Once we began to erect our copies of ancient monuments on site, and often far from engineers' offices and the source of raw materials, a fresh set of problems inevitably came up. Our archaeological experts did not always agree with the historical accuracy of the stonemasons' or engineers' schemes. The engineers, it turned out, were often less practically minded than they liked to admit. We had expected the second of these glitches, and always brought along as close a modern equivalent as we could find to an ancient foreman. The result was not welcomed by our building teams, but was a bonus for us film-makers: disagreement is always a good ingredient in a documentary. There were certainly some strong words and a good deal of tension. My experience of building sites today is that arguments about how to get the job done are frequent; I am certain that the same thing happened on Peruvian mountain tops, by the Tiber and the Nile and on the Wiltshire Downs, whether it was five hundred or four thousand years ago.

It was difficult for our construction teams to realize that we were not there to rebuild the Ancient World, but to record an experimental attempt to show how it might have been done. Of course we were pleased when all the effort proved successful, but that did not necessarily make the best film! Failure can be as interesting as success, and it can often be more informative. Nevertheless, taking all our experiments together we succeeded in some cases, although not without sweat and the threat of failure, as this book records. In others we did indeed fail to achieve what our ancient forebears did so well. It is a salutary lesson that in another thousand years their monuments will probably still be standing, while the best that we can hope for our experiments is that they will remain in a library and a mouldering videotape vault. One outcome of making these films is that they have increased our respect for our ancestors, regardless of where they lived on the planet.

STONEHENGE

CYNTHIA PAGE

STONEHENGE is one of the most remarkable achievements of prehistoric engineering in Europe, and the effort and commitment involved in its construction was equivalent to that of putting man on the moon in our own century. Yet it is one of the world's most mysterious, most enigmatic places, because so little is known about it. Nobody knows why it was built, who built it, nor how it was built.

It was constructed on Salisbury Plain in southern England during a period when the people living in Britain, Ireland and northern France were moving and erecting huge stones and building massive earthworks. These projects, which involved tremendous communal effort, were being carried out between roughly 3500 BC and 1500 BC.

A UNIQUE MONUMENT

There are about a thousand stone circles in the British Isles and over twelve hundred in northern France, which vary in size and shape. Some are relatively simple, consisting of stones which appear to have been lying close by and have been dragged upright. At Callanish, in the remote Outer Hebrides off the coast of

Stonehenge: the almost perfect sets of concentric circles and the inner horseshoe of shaped stones make it a unique monument.

Scotland, the circle is quite small but forms a spectacular arrangement of tall, thin stones. Others, like the one at Avebury in Wiltshire, are far grander. Avebury comprises a massive ditch inside a bank which is nearly a mile in circumference, and today encloses not only part of the village of Avebury but also a circle of huge standing stones. Carnac in northern France is even more impressive, with twelve parallel lines of stones running for over 950 metres. But Stonehenge is unique: it is the only stone monument that has been built with such skill, such effort and such dedication. What we see at Stonehenge today is the ruin of a temple that was started in about 2000 BC and took some three hundred years to build; it was abandoned in about 1500 BC. It is made up of a circle of massive upright stones which are linked together with a ring of horizontal lintels. Inside the circle is a horseshoe arrangement of five sets of even larger stones arranged as trilithons (two upright stones topped with a lintel). Just to make things more complicated, there is another set of smaller stones inside the circle which mirror the arrangement of the larger stones. Other isolated stones are set outside the circle.

The arrangement of the stones is complicated to describe because Stonehenge is not the result of a single big building effort. Archaeologists have divided its history into three phases. The first took place about five thousand years ago and consisted of a big ditch and bank with a wooden temple in the middle. This was followed a thousand years later by two separate building phases involving two sets of stones, one of relatively small stones, the other of much larger ones which were put up at different times.

RE-CREATING THE GREAT TRILITHON

These days it is quite difficult for the average visitor to work out, from what looks like a rather haphazard arrangement of stones, how Stonehenge might have looked in 1500 BC. Some stones have fallen over, others are broken and yet others have been taken away.

Many visitors are disappointed, the most common complaint being, 'It's smaller than I thought.' If only they were allowed to step over the rope, walk the few metres into the stone circle and stand near the stones, they would come away astounded at the size. The biggest stone weighs over 40 tonnes and is 9 metres long: it towers 7 metres above the ground with another 2 metres under the ground. Situated in the inner horseshoe of stones, forming part of the Great Trilithon, the huge stone now stands alone since its partner fell down and broke over two hundred years ago.

The *Secrets of Lost Empires* team decided to re-create the Great Trilithon – only the biggest stones would provide enough of a challenge! We would tackle the mystery of how these huge stones could be man-handled across the country-side, and then put upright, and finally how a massive lintel stone was put on the top. Using ancient tools, we would try to do something that had not been done for three and a half thousand years.

What makes Stonehenge so remarkable is that it was built at a time which spans the Neolithic period, which came at the end of the Stone Age, and the subsequent Bronze Age. During the Neolithic period, which in Britain lasted from about 4000 BC to 2000 BC, the only practical tools were of stone, wood or bone. Even at the beginning of the Bronze Age, a period which lasted until about 800 BC, the newly available metal was not only far too soft to be used for tools but it was also far too scarce and precious.

The task of moving and erecting the stones was given to engineer Mark Whitby, with archaeologist Julian Richards on hand to see that the methods were kept as authentic as possible. Mark would only be able to use tools that Julian told him were available three to four thousand years ago. There were no pulleys, no cranes and no metal tools. However, he would be able to use modern tools once he had proved that the ancient method worked. For example, once he proved it possible to move the stone, he would not have to pull it all the way to Stonehenge.

Mark Whitby is a structural engineer – very simply, he works with architects to make sure that designs which look good on paper don't fall down when they are built. He was asked to help on the project because he is extremely creative and imaginative. This was a very stimulating quality during the planning stages because he had so many fresh ideas, but less so when all the planning was finished and he was still coming up with new ways of moving the stone!

The remaining stone of the Great Trilithon at
Stonehenge. This was the stone that the *Secrets of Lost Empires*
team decided to replicate and transport.

Julian Richards is one of the few archaeologists who has practical experience of digging in the area: for him Stonehenge is a passion, and the challenge of moving the massive stones was a dream come true. Plenty of archaeologists had speculated about how these stones could be moved. But it was all talk – no one had actually had a go. There had been a successful experiment in the 1950s to move one of the small stones, but no one had attempted the big one. Yet anyone who visits Stonehenge gets the impression that this is the one question that the archaeologists have actually solved. Visitors are told exactly how the stones were moved and how they were put upright; there is no hint that there could be any alternative ways. The *Secrets* team set themselves the task of challenging the orthodox view and seeing if these ideas would really work.

Before the team could even start to work out how to move the stone they had to make a major decision: would they be allowed to use ropes? There is no archaeological evidence for the existence of rope so long ago, although a small piece of string, which is much thinner than rope, has been found in a Neolithic site in the east of England. Of course, that does not mean that there was no rope around when Stonehenge was built, because rope would have been made out of natural materials which rot, so evidence could never have been expected to survive. In any case it is very hard to think of a way of moving those massive stones without some form of rope. So Mark and Julian decided that ropes would be used. But what were they made of?

Jake Keen of the Dorset Ancient Technology Centre came to the rescue. Leather thongs were perfectly feasible, but he foresaw a big problem in making leather ropes that were long enough. There would be too many weak points where the strips of leather were knotted or tied together, and the stretch in such ropes would have been enormous. Plant fibres were much more likely to have been used, but the fibres had to be long if a good strong rope was to be made. Although stinging nettles have good fibres (and incidentally were still being used in the First World War by the Germans to make ropes to pull their guns) their fibres would be too short. The answer, according to Jake, was the small-leaf lime tree, and he was persuaded to test his theory. He stripped a 10-metre length of bark off a tree and put it in the mud of a river bed where it retted (an ancient word

for rotting) for six weeks. During that time bacteria in the mud destroyed every-thing in the bark except some very long, strong fibres which Jake plaited and twisted into a rope. When he tested a very simple rope it did surprisingly well – it finally broke under the strain of just under 1 tonne.

Julian and Mark were now convinced that using ropes would be historically accurate, but they decided to use modern ones made of natural fibres because no one had the time or money to make the amount of rope that would be needed from the small-leaf lime bark. There was also the question of safety: home-made ropes certainly would not have stood up to modern Health and Safety standards.

These days archaeologists can get a better idea of when Stonehenge was built and how long it took to build by using a technique called radiocarbon dating. All living things contain carbon, but along with this 'normal' carbon there is a radioactive version which is called an isotope. Living material contains the same amount of this isotope, but after an animal or plant dies it starts decaying at a known rate. So measuring the amount of radioactive carbon left in, for example, bones, antlers or charcoal found in the chalk at the bottom of the pits where the stones stand gives a good guide to when that stone was put in the hole.

There is a general agreement among archaeologists that Stonehenge probably started off in about 3100 BC when people started digging a big bank and a ditch in a rather featureless piece of land on the downlands of Salisbury Plain in south-west Britain. Why this site was chosen is a mystery – there seems to be nothing around to make it special. It lies below the brow of a small hill and even today most people driving down the A303 are surprised to find that the most famous Stone Age monument in the world is in what seems to be such an unin-teresting location.

Inside this ditch or henge the people built a big round wooden building. It was probably a temple or communal place of worship, because Stonehenge and the area around never seem to have been lived in – there are no traces of the usual rubbish that people leave behind and which is so useful for archaeologists. So this part of Salisbury Plain has always been a 'special place'.

The site with its wooden building probably lasted for about five hundred years and then it was abandoned for another five hundred. Even this early

Stonehenge included a few uncut large stones, but in about 2000 BC something radical happened – the area became so important that about eighty relatively small stones weighing up to 4 tonnes each were erected to form two concentric circles. These two stone circles were never finished. Someone must have decided to build something much bigger and better: a monument that would outshine anything ever seen before. The next three hundred years were spent making Stonehenge into the most impressive monument that Western Europe had ever seen. But the small stones were not discarded – they were incorporated into the bigger complex arrangement of stones.

THE BLUESTONE CONTROVERSY

Somehow it is not surprising that they kept these small stones, called bluestones. Although they are dwarfed by the much larger ones, and most visitors barely notice them, they have created one of the great mysteries that surround Stonehenge. There are no known sources of bluestone anywhere in the vicinity. A survey in the 1920s of all the possible outcrops found that the very closest source was in the Preseli mountains in the far west of Wales, over 120 miles away. The puzzle is, how did the eighty-two bluestones get to Stonehenge? Controversy has raged over this conundrum for more than a hundred years.

There are two theories – either the stones were brought to the Salisbury Plain area by glacial action, or people brought them from Wales. The Victorians were the first to suggest that the stones had arrived via a glacier. But in the 1920s it was suggested that the stones could only have been brought by humans because there was no evidence that the glaciers which had travelled across Wales had ever reached as far as the Salisbury Plain area. Human transport remained more or less in favour for the next forty years. Then, in the 1960s, the glacier theory came out of the woodwork and has been lurking ever since. Meanwhile, the human transport supporters remained loyal to their cause.

At last in 1991 the matter appeared to be settled once and for all. A paper called 'The Geological Sources and Transport of the Bluestones of Stonehenge,

Wiltshire, UK' by Richard Thorpe and his colleagues, was published. It was the result of extremely thorough and exciting research and the paper became head-line news. Here was the proof that the glacier theory supporters had been waiting for. After several years negotiating with the Stonehenge authorities, the scientists had been given permission to take samples from fifteen of the bluestones. Using modern geochemical analysis they compared these samples with outcrops of bluestones in the Preseli mountains. They used a technique called X-ray fluores-cence, which gave them a chemical 'fingerprint' of each sample. As the rocks from each outcrop contain slightly different chemical elements, this meant that they could identify where each sample from Stonehenge had come from.

The word bluestone is slightly misleading because it implies one sort of stone. In fact, there are several different rock types – spotted dolorites, rhyolites, volcanic ash and even sandstones. Some of them aren't even very blue, but for years it has been a convenient term to describe all the stones that come from the Welsh mountains.

One of the most thrilling moments during the research for the programme was being on top of an outcrop called Carn Menyn in the Preseli mountains, knowing that its stones had a direct link with the ones at Stonehenge. It was a typical midsummer day and the mist and rain made it very cold. Occasionally the mist cleared and big mounds of stones, which look as if they have just been thrown together, could be seen covering the tops of the hills. No matter how the stones had got to Stonehenge this outcrop was something special.

Several of the Stonehenge bluestones come from the Carn Menyn outcrop, while the origins of the rest are scattered over quite a large area. Some come from another outcrop close by, some from 20 miles away and one sample did not match up with any of the outcrops. At last their source had been not only positively identified but actually pinpointed. The conclusion was that only a glacier could have picked up such a ragbag of stones and carried them to the Stonehenge area.

Many of the human transport lobby were now won over into the glacial camp – but not all. The supporters of human transport ask why, if these distinctive stones were brought such a distance by a glacier, are there no bluestones left in the area around Stonehenge? Was every single one used to build Stonehenge? Have

The bluestones. Their origin is one of the great
mysteries of Stonehenge as the nearest source of these small stones is
in the Preseli mountains in south-west Wales.

they all been cleared away by farmers? There are no bluestones in any of the local buildings, and one diligent scientist even scoured the rivers in the whole of the Salisbury Plain area looking for evidence of glacial material. He looked at over 50 000 pebbles and found nothing that was foreign to the area: there was not a trace of a bluestone.

So why would the early Stonehenge builders have bothered to travel such a long distance to collect this odd mixture of stones? They are not even very good for building monuments: some of the bluestones at Stonehenge are quite soft and have weathered down to mere stumps. One glacier supporter wrote that dragging these stones such a way showed 'a liking for the blue-grey rock which bordered on insanity'.

Routes showing the way that the bluestones may
have been transported from the Preseli mountains.

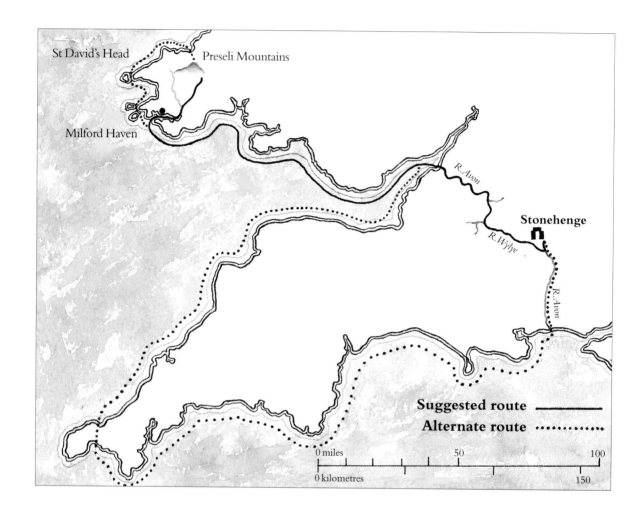

St David's Head

Preseli Mountains

Milford Haven

R.Avon

Stonehenge

R.Wylye

R.Avon

Suggested route ———
Alternate route ••••••••••

0 miles   50   100
0 kilometres   150

The human transport lobby, of course, disagree. They say that maybe these stones were worth the effort. The people who built Stonehenge were not living in an isolated world – they already had strong trading links with Wales and Ireland. Stone axes that could only have come from Wales have been found in the area. And the people in Wales were building stone monuments at least a thousand years before the bluestones were erected at Stonehenge. So maybe these bluestones were already very special. Maybe they were already part of a sacred stone circle. Maybe they were bought as a 'job lot' and it was this entire stone circle that was moved from Wales to Stonehenge.

In 1994 the glacier enthusiasts had another setback when one of the blue-stones from Stonehenge was dated using a new method. When a rock is exposed to the atmosphere for the first time, either by erosion or by quarrying, it starts to accumulate an isotope of chlorine. Measuring the amount of this isotope gives the date when it was first exposed. In this instance the results showed that the blue-stone rock from Stonehenge was only exposed about 14 000 years ago. Since the last Ice Age when glaciers would have been on the move was about 400 000 years ago the human transport lobby are now back in favour. The debate still has plenty of life in it and should continue for some time.

No matter which side one takes in the argument there is no doubt that the people who built this early phase of Stonehenge went to enormous lengths to get the stones. Even if a glacier had brought the stones to Salisbury Plain, the builders must have scoured the area and used every available bluestone.

MODERN PROBLEMS

Stonehenge is different from all other known stone monuments because it was built in an area without stones. The big stones that form the distinctive circle, the ones that everyone notices when they look at Stonehenge, are made of an incred-ibly hard sandstone called sarsen. It is the hardest rock in Britain, harder than granite, and is usually found lying around as big slabs. It is not the sort of stone that is ever quarried. Great slabs of this sarsen were deposited about 20–30 million years ago when the climate in what was to become the British Isles was tropical and balmy. The slabs eroded and broke up and moved down into valley bottoms where they can still be found.

Deposits of sarsens are scattered over the whole of southern Britain. It is excellent for building – even Windsor Castle is made of sarsen. But the Salisbury Plain area is bereft of decent large sarsens suitable for building monuments. Of course, since sarsens make such good building blocks, some people argue that they have all been used up. Yet, just like the bluestones, there are no sarsen stones in any of the buildings in the villages near Stonehenge. The nearest place to find them is over 20 miles to the north on the Marlborough Downs. This does not compare with the source of the bluestones, but it is still a very long way to bring a 40-tonne stone.

The first task for the team was to find a 40-tonne stone – understandably English Heritage, the custodians of Stonehenge, were reluctant to allow us to move one of the real stones. It soon became obvious that using a stone made out of sarsen was not going to be possible. There are still slabs of big sarsens lying around in valleys in the Marlborough Downs, but the fact that they were not big enough was not the only problem.

Most of the stones are protected and have been designated Sites of Special Scientific Interest because they are covered with rare species of lichens. The only thing to do was to make the stones out of concrete, and it was probably the only easy decision of the whole project.

The next hurdle to be tackled was where to build the Great Trilithon. 'Aim for the top' is the golden rule of making television programmes. The chairman of English Heritage thought that recreating the Great Trilithon was a brilliant idea, and one of their archaeologists even helped select a site only 200 metres away from the famous stones. It all seemed too easy and of course never happened; but it took English Heritage seven months to say no! So three weeks before filming was due to start there was no site for the stones.

So the hunt began for a suitable site. Again, it seemed like an easy task. Stonehenge is surrounded by land belonging to the Ministry of Defence and the local army base was already being generous in letting us use some land to build our replica stones. A suitable piece of waste land was found. It had a decent slope over which to pull the stones and a flattish area to erect them. The only problem was that we would be filming over several weekends. And those just happened to be the weekends when the Territorial Army was booked in for artillery practice. It would have sounded as if we were in the middle of a world war!

At last we found a cooperative farmer who didn't mind sacrificing a corner of his field. If you looked carefully you could just about see Stonehenge in the distance. It seemed a good compromise. Just as a precaution we thought we should tell the local police what we were up to, as the site was quite near the main road. No problem, said the police, but when are you planning this? There was a slight hesitation when the first three weekends of June were mentioned. Then the answer came – it was a very firm no.

A special Act of Parliament gives the local Wiltshire police extraordinary powers: they are allowed to close the roads around Stonehenge at a moment's notice for most of the month of June. And if hordes of people appear they cordon off the whole area. These special powers are to prevent any New Age travellers from congregating in the area during the Summer Solstice which, for many people, is the most significant time in the Stonehenge calendar.

Eventually the network of local archaeologists found us a field. Just like the Stonehenge site, it had a thin layer of topsoil covering solid chalk. Again, like Stonehenge, it was on rolling downlands. And, although it was 20 miles away from Stonehenge, at least it was on the Marlborough Downs close to the source of the big sarsens. Somehow it felt like the right place to be – it felt authentic.

WANDERING GARDENERS

The unremarkable location of such a remarkable building as Stonehenge is explained by the fact that the area itself was special long before the stone circles were built, long before the bluestone phase, even before the ditch and wooden building. In 1980 Julian Richards was digging in the area roundabout when he made an amazing discovery. He and his fellow archaeologists were investigating a henge – a Neolithic circular ditch – on a hill just south of Stonehenge. They had done some geophysical surveys and were measuring the magnetic resistance in the soil, which is a very good, quick method for finding the outline of ditches. They found the ditch that they were looking for, but there was something else on the printout just outside the henge that looked interesting. And, as Julian says, 'any good archaeologist has got to be nosy'. So he started digging.

What he uncovered was a deep pit, and in all his years as an archaeologist he had never seen anything like it. The assortment of flint tools, charcoal, pottery and bones that it contained was staggering. There were over two thousand fragments of bone from cattle, pigs, roe deer, red deer, beaver and trout. It was obvious that everything had been eaten, because some of the big bones had been smashed to get at the marrow. The pottery, and there were 1375 bits of 41 pots, was some of the oldest found in Britain – nearly six thousand years old. All of it had been deliberately smashed. This was a very special find, but what made it even more special was that this was no ordinary rubbish dump from an ancient settlement. Julian had excavated the remains from one huge party. Radiocarbon dating showed that the pit had been filled in around 3800 BC, and judging from the number of immature animal bones the feast was in the summer. A vast amount of food was eaten, but it wasn't all finished. Only the roe deer was completely eaten. The rest was probably taken away to be eaten later. Is this the first evidence for a prehistoric doggy bag? So about a thousand years before Stonehenge was even thought of, groups of people were coming together, maybe to gossip, to check on the best hunting grounds or even to find sexual partners.

'Wandering gardeners' is one description of the early settlers of Salisbury Plain. In those days the area would have been heavily wooded, and the hunter gatherers who had roamed the area for centuries would have begun to settle down for short periods, planting and harvesting corn and then moving on. Eventually these groups would have established their hunting grounds and planting areas, as well as rights of movement across neighbouring territories.

Long before Stonehenge was built, the early settlers were establishing boundaries. Mounds of earth – long barrows – were built at strategic points to be easily seen. A tremendous amount of effort went into these mounds, and not far from Stonehenge lies a barrow that is over 100 metres long. These days the barrows merge with the landscape, but when they were built they must have been real landmarks of gleaming white chalk. Some of these mounds eventually took on a greater significance within the scattered community. They became places of burial, not for individuals but for whole communities.

The very impressive West Kennet long barrow stands about 20 miles from Stonehenge on the top of a hill and is 110 metres long – one of the biggest in Britain. It is about a thousand years older than Stonehenge and the entrance to the tomb is fascinating. Huge boulders have been dragged up the hill and built into the entrance to form a crude version of the stone arches that were later built at Stonehenge. Forty-seven bodies were found inside the chamber, and the distribution of the bones shows how the 'wandering gardeners' were developing into a structured society which had strong links with its past. There are five stone chambers in the tomb. Bones of children, women and the elderly were found in the smaller chambers. The biggest chamber contained only the bones of adult males. So, although children, women and the elderly were seen as valued members of this society, there is no doubt who the most important members were.

For some unknown reason it looks as if the occupants were not put in the tomb as complete dead bodies. Instead, bundles of bones which had already been buried elsewhere and had been allowed to decompose were brought to the tomb. Maybe these bodies decomposed naturally or maybe they had been left out in the open for the elements or the birds to deflesh them – rather like the 'sky' burials in Tibet where bodies are left for the vultures to devour. But when it was time to take the bones to the tomb most of the smaller bones – the fingers and toes – were left behind. And they were not put in the tomb as separate bodies; instead, skulls were put in one place, long bones in another, and the rest shoved into a corner. But what is puzzling is that the number of skulls does not tally with the number of long bones. Maybe some of the skulls were removed to be used in a ceremony; or – and it is not too hard to imagine – a splinter group decided to move away to set up on their own, and took a few skulls as a tangible link with their ancestors.

So, a thousand years before Stonehenge was built, these burial chambers were serving not only as territorial markers but as meeting places for the community. The chambers show that this society was already segregated and that a hierarchy was well established. The tomb was in use for at least twenty-five generations, and probably only the bones of the more important members of the community were taken to the tomb.

The people of this part of southern Britain seemed to have developed a passion for making their mark on the landscape. At the bottom of the hill from the West Kennet tomb is one of the most amazing sights in all of ancient Britain: Silbury Hill. Completely man-made, it is huge and just as mysterious and impressive as Stonehenge. The hill has very steep sides over 40 metres high. The top is flat

BELOW Silbury Hill. The huge, mysterious, man-made
mound was built in the same way as the early Egyptian pyramids.
OPPOSITE Avebury, the oldest stone circle in Britain.

and is big enough to play a game of cricket. Excavations have shown that it was very carefully built in the same fashion as the very earliest of the stepped pyramids of Egypt. But it does not seem to be a tomb – no one knows what it was for.

PEOPLE POWER

There are more stone monuments in the area around Stonehenge than anywhere else in Europe, and by the time they came to erect Stonehenge the people who built it must have perfected a technique for moving these massive stones. Avebury, which is only 20 miles away, is the biggest stone circle in Britain. Several centuries

before the last building phase at Stonehenge, the people of Avebury were dragging the stones and up-ending them. They seem to have chosen stones that were naturally pillar-shaped, because none of these Avebury stones has been shaped. They did not have to look far for them – there are still a lot of sarsens in the valley nearby. But this is also the closest source of these large sarsen stones to Stonehenge, and so most archaeologists believe that the Stonehenge builders had to travel over 20 miles to the same valley to collect the stones for their monument.

The *Secrets* team had to decide on a method of moving their replica stones. Would they need animals? Some books have suggested that oxen might have been used. There were certainly no horses around at the time Stonehenge was built, but bones have been found of large cattle which would have been big enough to help pull a big stone. But did the people who built Stonehenge have the knowledge and husbandry to use them? Getting a team of oxen – castrated bullocks – to pull together efficiently is a very skilled operation, and oxen are not the easiest of animals to handle.

The team decided to tackle the challenge – especially as a team of oxen would look quite spectacular on film. So Britain was scoured for trained oxen. It was not a great success. Eventually two untrained oxen were tracked down and the farmer was very helpful. Yes, he could get some more oxen and train them to pull. But there was a small problem: it was going to take six months to train them, and it would cost almost the whole budget to do so! So it had to be people power. But before Mark Whitby could decide how many people he needed he had to decide on how he was going to pull the stones.

Everyone agreed that a 40-tonne stone cannot be pulled on its own across rough ground: the friction between stone and ground would be too great. Over the months of planning, Mark decided he wanted to replace the 40-tonne stone with a smaller, 10-tonne stone. But we would not let him have his way.

Moving a 10-tonne stone would have been difficult, but the 40-tonne stone would present a completely different set of problems. Pulling a 40-tonne stone isn't just four times harder than pulling a 10-tonne one, because of the unique way in which the larger stone interacts with the ground underneath: it can be literally 'sucked' down on to the ground.

It was never going to be an easy task. We had told Mark that there was no point in just moving it along a flat piece of ground because the area around Stonehenge is not flat. He had to show it being moved up a hill. The stone would have to be put on to a wooden sled. But what would that sled run on? Certainly not on unprepared ground. In most books, as well as on the information boards at Stonehenge, it is stated quite categorically, and with great authority, that the stones were put on sleds and dragged across the plain on rollers. This was a method which had been used very successfully in the only other experiment to have been carried out in an attempt to move Stonehenge-type stones.

In 1954 the debate on whether the bluestones had arrived from Wales by human power or by glaciers was having one of its periodic revivals. Professor

Richard Atkinson was at the time the undisputed authority on Stonehenge. Not convinced by the glacier theory, he decided to put the theory of human transport to the test. He borrowed some local schoolboys and had a block of concrete made which weighed about 1 tonne. His theory of how the stones could have been brought from Wales depended on a route that was partly overland and partly by water.

The experiment was a great success, and proved that the easiest way to move the stone was on water. When the stone was lashed on to a raft, a couple of boys were able to punt it quite easily along a shallow river. Where the river became deeper a small team of four boys pulling from the bank was all that was needed. Hauling the stone overland, however, needed more boys and much better co-ordination. The 1-tonne stone was put on a sled and dragged on the ground just down the hill from Stonehenge, which has a slope of 1:15. This needed thirty-two boys pulling as hard as they could. However, when wooden rollers were put under the sled, the task was much easier – only fourteen boys were needed for pulling. But ten boys were needed to shift the rollers and cope with the problems of steering the stone.

Professor Atkinson did not even contemplate moving a large sarsen, but on the basis of this experiment, he worked out that a huge 40-tonne stone would need a work force of 1000 men for the flattish parts of the journey and 1500 men when there were hills. Others have calculated that 460 were needed for the flat and 600 men for the hills. It was obviously an area of research that was wide open for a practical demonstration.

Mark had serious doubts about the orthodox view of rollers and insisted that before filming he should be allowed to carry out some tests, to which we reluc-tantly agreed. But these were the only preliminary tests he was allowed to make. Of course, engineers would not normally launch themselves into such a project without all sorts of tests on the computer and with scale models, but if all the problems had been sorted out before the filming started it would have made for a very dull programme. Mark was persuaded on the basis that 'you learn best when you watch someone else's mistakes' and that the aim of the programme was to see how Stonehenge was built – if he failed, it would not be disastrous.

The 1954 experiment by Professor Richard Atkinson
which involved teams of schoolboys transporting a 1-tonne stone
over ground and over water.

As it turned out, those tests proved to be invaluable. Rollers were fine for small and medium-weight blocks. But over 10 tonnes a problem arose: the rollers started to snag and bunch together. Mark needed to find a different way. Any idea of using wheeled transport was dismissed; there is archaeological evidence from Germany that the wheel had arrived in Europe by this time, but even today wheeled transport would not be used to move such a big weight over uneven ground.

First Mark thought about levering the stone up and 'walking' it along. This was a method that had been tried successfully in an experiment to move the great Easter Island statues, but he discarded it as being too labour-intensive. Then he thought about tipping the stone up and over. That was rejected on several grounds: it was too dangerous, too much like hard work, and during a 20-mile journey might have smashed the stone. Eventually he decided that the stone would be pulled on some sort of sled on a prepared track.

Mark's approach was to assume that there would only have been a small community of people, however dedicated, to move the sarsens. So he set about working out a system to move our stone with the minimum number of people. It was inspired by a trip to the seaside, where he had seen fishermen dragging their boat up the beach over a set of rollers. But the rollers were not rolling – there was a groove where the keel of the boat slid over, and this groove had grease on it. Now he was going to attempt to move the 40-tonne stone on a prepared, greased track. The track would be like two railway lines set into the ground and the grease would be the modern equivalent of tallow – animal fat which would certainly have been available to the builders of Stonehenge. The thinking behind this idea was that a small group of people could take their time preparing a track, after which the stronger members of the community would turn up and pull. The track could then be lifted and reused on the next section of the journey.

How on earth they organized this mammoth effort over the three hundred years it took to build Stonehenge is difficult to imagine. It was hard enough for the production team, armed with telephones and faxes, to find enough strong people to pull. Mark calculated that he needed two hundred. And as there was no money in the budget to pay this number of labourers it was decided to concentrate the action over three weekends and look for volunteers. All the obvious places – Army, Territorial Army, Navy, RAF, Duke of Edinburgh Award participants, police, fire brigade, ambulance service, rowing clubs, football clubs, rugby clubs, universities and colleges, local businesses, radio appeals, re-enactment societies, countryside organizations, Round Table, local pubs, Young Farmers, Venture Scouts and mountaineering societies – were tried. This – not pulling the stone and getting it upright – was perhaps the major achievement of the whole project. The last week before we were due to film began frantically. After hundreds of phone calls, on the day before filming started, we had a list of 220 men and women who had promised faithfully to help.

The first day of filming began in a rather tense way. The plan was to pull the 40-tonne stone up a 1:20 hill on the prepared track, but in order to get everyone into the swing of it the stone would first be pulled down the slope. The pullers were checked in as they arrived in dribs and drabs. But only 135 actually turned up. There were maybe just enough of them to pull the stone down the hill, but it was very doubtful if so few could manage to get the stone up it. It looked as if the whole project was doomed to failure before we had even started pulling.

The stone had already been put on to a wooden sled with runners which fitted on the two greased tracks. A piece of wood between the runners fitted between the tracks and kept the stone from being pulled sideways and off the track. The first pull was surprisingly easy: the huge stone glided almost effortlessly down the slope, gathering speed as it went. But the uphill pull was, of course, another story. The stone would not move. They pulled and pulled, and nothing moved. The problem did not, however, seem to be lack of strength on the part of the pullers. What had happened was that the sled had become stuck to the track – the grease had formed a bond which had to be broken before the stone could be shifted. They tried the battering ram technique: big wooden poles were banged against the back of the stone. It did not move. They tried levers. That did not work. They tried levering and pulling at the same time. Still no joy – it seemed that nothing was going to break the seal underneath.

Eventually, though, the people on the levers and the teams of pullers made one last supreme effort and the stone started to inch forward up the hill. And then something quite amazing happened. Everyone had assumed that if this small number of pullers did manage to move the stone it would be a slow and laborious process. What was surprising was that, once it did start moving, instead of inching its way up the slope, it moved quite quickly, starting slowly and gathering momentum – in fact it moved at a decent walking pace. Although the grease caused tremendous problems by sticking the stone to the track, once that bond was broken it allowed even a small team of men and women to move the great weight relatively easily.

Whether or not this system would work on the one big hill between the Marlborough Downs and Stonehenge was a problem that the team decided to leave for someone else to solve. How long the 20-mile journey would have taken was also difficult to calculate, because it would depend on how long it took for new sections of the track to be prepared. But at least we had shown that it was possible to move a 40-tonne stone up a hill.

By the time the final phase of Stonehenge was being built the society had changed from an egalitarian one into something much more hierarchical and structured. The concept of the big communal burial mound containing large numbers of people had gone. Instead, every hilltop around Stonehenge is now covered with individual burial mounds – round barrows. Each one of these mounds is the burial place of someone rich and powerful – they had to be important people to be buried so close to Stonehenge. But one of the barrows stands out from all the others, for buried in it is the richest and most important person associated with Stonehenge.

Bush Barrow was excavated at the beginning of the nineteenth century; inside were the bones of one individual who was described as 'a stout and tall man'. But the excavators were not interested in the bones and left them in the barrow, where they remain today. What they were interested in was what was buried with him. They found some absolutely incredible objects made of gold, the most impressive being a gold breast plate. Many people believe that this is the burial place of the man who built Stonehenge.

Although they had chiefs and maybe priests, nothing is known about the rest of the society – the ordinary people who helped build Stonehenge. Were they slaves or did they help willingly? Perhaps it was such a prestigious project that just being associated with it gave the builders a status within their community, and they didn't have to be coerced into helping. They may have been volunteers.

Nothing remains of their houses or settlements. The only clues to the identity of the Stonehenge builders come from the burial mounds around Stonehenge, which contain objects from all over Western Europe – pottery, beautiful jewellery fashioned from gold and amber, and stone and metal axes. Stonehenge seems to have been the focal point for the trading routes which ran between Ireland and the west of Britain, and the rest of Europe. Amber came from the Baltic, gold from Wales, tin from Cornwall and copper from Scandinavia,

Moving the replica 40-tonne stone: greasing the track;
the team of willing helpers; and the comparatively easy
downhill pull.

Ireland and the west of Britain. By about 2000 BC the secret of bronze – copper alloyed with tin – had been discovered, so during the period that Stonehenge was being built the new metal was known. But the bronze axes and tools were too valuable to be ever used and were for ceremonial purposes only. In fact, bronze is far too soft for cutting and shaping stones, or to be used in the making of weapons.

STANDING STONES

The next task for the team was to get the 40-tonne stone upright. Mark had decided that brute strength alone would not get the massive stone up, and he spent months tackling this problem – in fact he concentrated on it so much that the rest of the project rather suffered. He was being asked to tackle a problem using techniques which were four thousand years old but at the same time he had to observe the present-day safety regulations. The standard textbook way of raising the stone has people levering the stone and pushing blocks under it as they lift (see page 34). Mark was certain that this orthodox way would take far too long, be far too difficult and probably much too dangerous as well.

A vital clue was the shape of the holes in which the stones stand at Stonehenge – steep on one side and ramped on the other. That meant that the stone might well have been tipped into the hole, and Mark designed an ingenious way to re-enact this hypothesis. First, he had a ramp built next to the hole.

Neolithic people, incidentally, would have had no problems digging holes with antler horns as picks and the shoulder blades of cows or deer as spades; and a hole for one of the big sarsens would only have taken two or three days to prepare. These holes at Stonehenge are not a standard size – they vary in depth. This was because they could not find stones that were all of the same height, so they compensated by setting some of the stones in deeper holes than others. The reason that the Great Trilithon stone stands on its own is because its partner is much shorter and was buried in too shallow a hole.

The big replica stone was balanced on Mark's ramp. The front half was perched over the hole, and the stone's centre of gravity was just behind the edge of

BELOW LEFT The traditionally recognized way of erecting the
sarsen uprights at Stonehenge. BELOW RIGHT AND BOTTOM The team
dig a hole for their replica and succeed in dropping it in place.

Hauling the stone into an upright position proved to be a
difficult task until the big upright poles were replaced by a more
stable A-frame structure.

the hole. Mark's idea was to use the weight of the stone to get it into the hole. He was planning to do this by moving a weight along the top of the big stone. Six small stones were hauled up on to the back end of the big stone and strapped on to a small sled. The principle was that, as these smaller stones were pulled forward along the top of the big stone, their weight would shift the centre of gravity and make the front end of the big stone heavier and this extra weight would topple it into the hole.

It would be either Mark's greatest moment or the most public of failures – it had been tested out only in his office, using a ruler to demonstrate the principle. Nobody had ever done this in practice before (except, Mark claimed, the people who built Stonehenge). The stone had to fall into the hole exactly as planned. The hole had been dug to the exact dimensions of the one at Stonehenge, which was only slightly bigger than the stone itself. If the stone didn't fall straight, Mark was in trouble.

It was certainly the most exciting moment of the whole project, and it happened very quickly. One moment the huge stone was on its side, and the next it had plopped into its hole. It was a spectacular success.

The next stage should have been so easy. The stone was already three-quarters upright and all the team of pullers had to do was haul it into the final upright position. A straight pull was not possible as there weren't enough people. It turned out to be a day of unmitigated frustrations. Mark had devised a system of huge wooden poles which would work like giant levers and reduce the effort needed to pull the stone up. Ropes were attached from the top of the stone to the bottom of these wooden poles. Another set of ropes was attached to the top of these poles for the team of pullers to haul on. The pullers would move the top of the poles about 4 metres and the bottom of the pole would then move about 1 metre, transmitting this movement to the stone with about four times the force. That was the theory.

In the event it was a complete mess. The huge poles kept falling to one side and the pullers spent more time and effort keeping them upright than moving the stone. A whole day was wasted, during which the euphoria of getting the stone into the hole rapidly disappeared.

Mark eventually took some advice and converted his wooden poles into a much more stable structure – an A-frame. Ropes from the top of the stone were attached to the A-frame and at last, very, very slowly, the stone started to move. After much heaving it was gradually pulled upright. Although Mark was suffering from hurt pride, the tremendous effort needed to move the stone into the final upright position justified his method for tilting the stone into the hole.

There had been a few murmurs of it being too much of a twentieth-century, over-engineered approach. But Julian Richards had been convinced that Mark's method was a possibility. He believes that the people who built Stonehenge were very sophisticated and obviously capable of thinking up great schemes; and that as they were hauling the big stones over a period of at least three hundred years it is more than likely that someone would have thought up easier ways of doing things.

CRAFTSMEN-CARPENTERS

It is quite staggering to think that Stonehenge was built, when the only tools available were of stone or bone, by people who achieved a perfection that had never been seen before in any other stone monument in Europe. Stonehenge is the only stone monument from the whole of the Neolithic and the early Bronze Ages in which each stone has been cut and shaped.

They must have been excellent carpenters, because they used techniques which are still used today. It could be that Stonehenge is a stone version of the wooden building which was there before the stones. At the top of the big uprights there is a carved bump; this is the tenon, which fits into the mortise – the hole in the lintel – to hold the lintel on top of the upright. And at the end of some of the lintels there are tongue-and-groove joints which hold the lintels in place. The accuracy is amazing. Stonehenge is actually built on a slope yet the lintels line up perfectly with each other. If the circle had ever been finished it would have been out by only 15 centimetres. The lintels in the outer circle are also slightly curved to make the circle more effective.

Cutting and shaping the sarsen stones was a task that the *Secrets* team decided not to tackle. Fortunately, experiments had already been done in which a professional stonemason had shown how it was possible to shape them using stone tools. One estimate reckons that it would have taken twenty-five men fifteen years to complete the task. It is a very long, tedious, difficult job. Since sarsens are so hard, shaping them would be a back-breaking job even using modern tools. But the experimenters had to use stone-battering balls – also made of sarsen - called mauls, some only the size of a cricket ball, others the size of footballs, to pound away at the surface in the same way that their distant ancestors would have done. The noise of the constant bashing day after day must have been horrendous.

Not only was each stone in the Great Trilithon made square, but the upright pillars were tapered so that they are slimmer at the top. This technique, also used by the Greeks, has the effect of making the pillars look much taller. Shaping the tenon at the top of the upright would have taken several weeks of work, and even more weeks of work would have been required to pound out the corresponding holes in the lintel after the two uprights were in place. But sometimes they made mistakes in their calculations, and the big lintel that belongs to the Great Trilithon has a permanent reminder of one of these miscalculations. There are two holes on the bottom side of the lintel, but on the top side are two more holes that were never finished. Someone must have realized that the first set of holes was in the wrong place and that the lintel was not going to fit on to the uprights. Imagine the day when that person told the workers that they had to scrap what they had done so far and start all over again on the other side! A less prosaic theory is that the holes were deliberate and that Stonehenge was originally a double-decker.

TOPPING THE TRILITHON

Getting the lintel on top of the uprights was the final task for the *Secrets* team. The second of the uprights was put into its hole with a big crane; then Mark had a choice of two methods for positioning the lintel, for the archaeological world is divided on how the original builders got it in place.

The impressive curved lintels on top
of the outer circle stones at Stonehenge.

One method is to build a big ramp and drag the lintel up it. The other is to make a timber platform or crib: the lintel is levered up at one end while timber beams are shoved underneath; then the other end is levered up and more timber is put under the lintel so that gradually the timber platform is built up underneath the stone. This is the preferred method and the one on display at Stonehenge.

By now Roger Hopkins had joined the team from America. He is the stone-mason who attempted to rebuild an Egyptian pyramid and to raise an Egyptian obelisk in other programmes in this series (see chapters 2 and 3). Roger had had a lot of experience moving large blocks of stones, and was particularly keen to try the timber crib method. He and a small team set up an experiment using old railway sleepers in place of the timber beams. It worked very well, although it was slow – but that would not have been a problem for the Stonehenge builders. It was interesting to watch the learning curve of the small team: at first they struggled with the levers and the timbers, but within a few hours they had got a very good system working. However, the team soon ran out of railway sleepers and it became obvious that a vast number of logs would have been needed to get the lintel to the top of the uprights. It would have been fascinating to see how this system worked when the lintel was 7 metres up, but there was neither the time nor the money to carry on with it. Mark therefore decided to try the alternative method, which he had been considering anyway.

Despite the fact that Julian Richards regards the timber crib as the more likely method, Mark felt it would be more dramatic to drag the lintel up a ramp. Again, budget and time considerations meant that this ramp could not be built using earth, so modern scaffolding tubes were used as a substitute. It was a huge ramp and it looked dreadful. And it was made even worse because all sorts of handrails were needed for safety reasons. It certainly did not have a prehistoric look about it. But the basic idea was the same, and Mark was not, after all, trying to prove that ramps could have been built by the people of Stonehenge. He was working on the same principle that he had used for dragging the stone: he believed that a big ramp of earth or even timber could be built slowly over several weeks or even months by a small team of people, and that the stronger members of the community would only be summoned for the great pull.

Having moved the 40-tonne stone, Mark and his team should have found a 9-tonne lintel easy work. It wasn't. Mark hoped that he had enough people to pull the stone up the ramp without the help of an A-frame. It didn't work – 9 tonnes is still a very heavy weight, especially up a steep ramp. They pulled and heaved but nothing worked. All that happened was that the ropes stretched and the pullers got exhausted. So Mark had to go back to using an A-frame to reduce the amount of effort. This worked well, but was slow.

The lintel was eventually hauled up 7 metres into the air. But even when it had reached the top Mark's problems were not over. There was almost a catastrophe when it was pulled too fast from the slope on to the flat area and thudded into the top of the two uprights with such force that the entire scaffolding shuddered and moved. And it was out of line with the top of the uprights. Getting the lintel in place was a nightmare. Tempers were frayed and near-anarchy set in, as by then everyone had a separate opinion on how to move it those final few centimetres. But what joy when it was done.

A MONUMENTAL CALENDAR?

The main mystery surrounding Stonehenge is not the details of its building so much as its purpose. The stones were dragged huge distances, after which a tremendous amount of time and labour was put into shaping them and getting them upright. Such a huge communal effort had to be for the whole community, and it had to be for a temple. But a temple to whom or what?

There have been more suggestions, more books written and more television programmes made about what Stonehenge was for than about any other monument in Europe. The truth is that no one knows. The people who built Stonehenge left very few clues. There are no writings, no hieroglyphs to decipher, not even any drawings; we only have some pottery, some grave goods and, of course, Stonehenge itself. But one thing can be stated quite categorically: Stonehenge has absolutely nothing whatsoever to do with the Druids. The Druids are priests belonging to a very ancient religion but they did not originate until the late Iron Age, long after Stonehenge was finished. The modern-day Druids belong to an eighteenth-century cult who have 'acquired' Stonehenge, and every year they attempt to hold their Midsummer Solstice ceremony at the stones.

No one knows what Stonehenge looked like when it was being used for the ceremonies that must have taken place. Maybe there was a wooden roof; maybe it was brightly painted or hung with garlands of flowers and branches. But what was it used for? The simplest and possibly the most acceptable theory is that Stonehenge marks the passage of time.

The one thing which is known for sure is that the stones are aligned to mark the Midsummer and Midwinter Solstices. At dawn on 21 June anyone standing inside the circle of stones and looking out would see the sun rise over a single stone, the Heel Stone, which is set apart from the rest of the circle. For most people this is the most significant day of the Stonehenge calendar, and it is certainly the day that gets the most attention from the public and the press. Yet it is possibly the Midwinter Solstice that is more important. For this you need to be on the outside, looking inwards. On 21 December it is the setting sun which drops down the side of the one remaining upright of the Great Trilithon. If the trilithon

The big ramp with the lintel at the bottom; the 'tenons' or
carved bumps at the top of the main stones; and the final difficult and
dangerous step – guiding the lintel into position.

The replica Great Trilithon with the scaffolding removed.
The *Secrets* team have donated it to English Heritage where it will be
a feature in the new visitors' centre.

were complete, the sun would be exactly in the middle of the two uprights. In many ways, marking the shortest day of the year has far more significance in an agricultural community. Imagine the power of the select few who had the knowledge, who could tell the rest of the community that the sun would now return, the days would get longer and it would soon be time to sow their crops.

Although Stonehenge is unique in so many ways, it is not the only monument to be aligned with the solstices; many others have similar alignment. A discovery in Ireland in the 1960s showed that a monument far older than Stonehenge had been built to mark the movement of the sun. Newgrange is one of the world's oldest buildings. It is a tomb made of over 200 000 tonnes of stone and is at least a thousand years older than the very earliest phase of Stonehenge. Although it has been a tourist attraction for three hundred years, no one had realized that it was far more than just a long passage leading to a dark tomb.

Michael O'Kelly was one of Ireland's leading archaeologists. He and his wife Claire were restoring the tomb when they came across a curious rectangular slit above the entrance that had apparently never been noticed. There were scratches on the stone that did not look natural; these marks looked as if the stone had been moved backwards and forwards yet the hole was far too small for anyone to climb through. Tradition had it that the sun shone into the tomb at midsummer, but the tomb was not orientated towards the north-east, so this was impossible.

Back home, Michael mulled over the discovery and then decided to drive to the tomb to spend the night there. It lies at the end of a 20-metre passage and there is, he says, an 'extraordinary sense of darkness'. It was at dawn that

> *I was literally astounded. The light began as a thin pencil and widened to a band of about 6 inches. There was so much light reflected from the floor that I could walk around inside without a lamp and avoid bumping off the stones. It was so bright I could see the roof 20 feet above me. And then after a few minutes the shaft of light narrowed as the sun appeared to pass westward across the slit and total darkness came once more.*

It was the morning of 21 December, the Midwinter Solstice.

AFTER STONEHENGE

The building of Stonehenge was one of the greatest visual statements ever made in Britain. A project that was designed to impress, it was the last and the greatest of the stone monuments of Western Europe. In about 1500 BC it was all over. Stonehenge was no longer the most important, the most special place in Britain. There was a decline in trade, and Stonehenge as a ceremonial place declined as well. Also, the sense of community was lost. There were no more burials near Stonehenge. The people drifted away into the valleys where they became farmers.

When the Romans invaded southern Britain in 55 and 54 BC, Stonehenge had been abandoned for 1500 years and was a ruin. Yet the Romans must have felt the power of the monument, as they appear to have avoided it. There are no pieces of Roman pottery for about a mile around the stones.

So what happened to the replica Great Trilithon? When the scaffolding was taken down it looked so magnificent that the farmer decided to keep it. The *Secrets* team were delighted, and even started the process of obtaining planning permission. But a week later there was a panic call from the farmer. The local police had warned him that a giant 'rave' party was being organized and that his land would be invaded by thousands of 'drug-crazy' people. Already the new trilithon was a focus of attention. The outcome was that it was taken down immediately and given to English Heritage for their new visitors' centre. But there is a long-standing conflict about where it is to be sited. So the three huge stones are back where they started – on a piece of waste land in the middle of an army base.

No one was claiming that the methods used by the *Secrets* team were the actual ones used by the Stonehenge builders. But what they did show was one way in which it could have been done, and that the Stonehenge builders could, through trial and error, have devised some ingenious ways to move their stones.

The final words have to be for the teams of pullers. At the beginning of the project it was touch and go, as so few of those who had promised to help turned up. By the final weekend it was the opposite – there were far too many people willing to help. Just like the Ancient Britons, they had been sucked into the aura and excitement of being involved in a mammoth project.

THE PYRAMID

MARK LEHNER

ABOUT 4700 years ago (2700 BC), the Ancient Egyptians began to build the world's first skyscrapers: the pyramid tombs of their Pharaohs. More than mortal kings, each ruler was seen as an incarnation of the god Horus, whose symbol the falcon soared above all living creatures. So the pyramids stood, like medieval cathedrals, at the centre of the society and economy of their time.

The geometry of a pyramid is simple – four points making the square of the base, a centre point raised to form the apex, and four triangular sloping faces. The standard pyramid complex included a temple at the centre of the eastern base where the Pharaoh's funeral took place, but also where daily rituals, including processions out of and around the pyramid, perpetuated the worship of the god-king. From the mortuary temple a causeway, with walls and a roof, ran down the plateau to end at the valley temple, the only entrance into the whole complex.

The low rectangular tombs called *mastabas* that surrounded the pyramid were households of the dead, whose continued prosperity in the afterlife depended, as in this life, on the household of the king. At the time when they built their largest pyramids, the Egyptians were developing the art of mummification. They preserved the earthly form of their dead as linen effigies lying in

The pyramids of Giza seen from the south-west, looking north-east.
FRONT Menkaure. CENTRE Khafre. REAR Khufu.

rock chambers under the *mastabas;* these were equipped with small offering chapels that formed a link with the land of the living.

The Great Pyramid of Khufu (or Cheops as he was known to the Greeks) remained the biggest building in the world until the early twentieth century AD. Within this king's thirty- or forty-year reign (*c.*2586–2551 BC) the builders set over 2 300 000 blocks of stone, weighing on average 2½ tonnes, to a height of 146.5 metres. The base covers 5.29 hectares, levelled to within about 2 cm around its perimeter. The sides are oriented to north, south, east and west, leaving at most 1.1 metres deviation. The largest discrepancy in the length of the sides is only 4.4 cm. How these ancient builders quarried, hauled, and set 6 million tonnes of stubborn rock into a mountain-sized pyramid of such precision without the pulley, wheel or modern transport baffled archaeologists for generations.

In search of answers I joined Roger Hopkins, a stonemason from Sudbury in Massachusetts, and the rest of the team in Egypt. Our plan was to test some of the more likely construction theories by building a small pyramid in the shadow of the Great Pyramid. We knew this would not be a 100 per cent replication of ancient technology, for our pyramid production had to fit within our film production schedule. This only allowed us about three weeks of quarrying and assembling materials and three weeks of actual building, which meant that the team had to forego testing certain major operations. For example, the stone was transported from the quarry by means of flat-bed diesel trucks rather than the barges that plied the Nile and its canals. In addition, Roger brought in a front-end loader to speed up the construction so that we would have time to test operations specific to the highest part, where working space is rapidly reduced as the pyramid approaches its apex. The forward scoops of these powerful wheeled machines are normally used for digging and pushing dirt. Roger used it as a crane for lifting and manoeuvring limestone blocks slung from steel cables. Our masons used iron hammers, chisels and levers; their ancient counterparts probably used only copper chisels and punches. After the time of what is known as the Old Kingdom (that is, after about 2181 BC), the Egyptians used bronze, an alloy of copper with 8-10 per cent tin, which is harder than pure copper. We tried out both copper and bronze tools. All our experiments were aimed at setting the stage for more authentic trials of specific ancient tools, techniques and operations.

THE ORIGIN OF THE PYRAMIDS

Ancient Egyptian civilization lasted from 3000 BC until the death of Cleopatra VII in 30 BC, after which Egypt became a province of the Roman Empire. Egyptologists divide this immense span of time into three 'kingdoms' separated by intermediate periods of collapse. The Egyptians made the largest stone pyramids in the Old Kingdom. They continued to build pyramids, mostly of mudbrick, in the Middle Kingdom. The New Kingdom is the age of empire when Pharaohs such as Tutankhamen and Ramses the Great made their tombs in the Valley of the Kings.

Ancient Egyptian history is further divided into thirty dynasties – ruling families or households. Dynasty 1 marks the emergence of pharaonic civilization under a unified kingdom around 3000 BC. This is the time of the earliest hieroglyphic writing and the first monumental architecture, consisting of rectangular mudbrick *mastaba* tombs for the most important people of the time. In only three hundred years, the Egyptians progressed from mudbrick to stone for building pyramids.

It was the Nile that made pyramid building possible. Fine limestone, granite, workers and provisions all arrived at a harbour at the foot of the plateau. Indeed, the Nile made civilization possible. Egypt, shaped like a papyrus plant with the delta as the head of the long stalk of the Nile Valley, is essentially a linear oasis flanked by the natural protection of the desert. Located at the centre of the land, the connection between valley and delta, the colossal early pyramids helped focus Egypt's kingdom and its resources into the world's first territorial nation-state.

This coordination of core and periphery is marked by the first pyramid, built around 2700 BC for the Pharaoh Djoser at Saqqara, about 12 miles south of Giza. The visionary Imhotep, Djoser's architect and high priest of the sun god,

Construction of the pyramids; a coloured engraving of 1862
shows teams of slaves hauling up the stones at a building site.

Ra at Heliopolis, conceived this first attempt to reach for the heavens. It was
Imhotep who first used stone instead of mudbrick to build a square *mastaba*
above the king's burial shaft. He realized that with this durable material he could
create a gigantic stepped mound, a kind of ladder by which the king's soul could
ascend to heaven. The outline of the Step Pyramid is, in fact, the hieroglyphic for
the verb 'to ascend'.

BELOW RIGHT Ancient Egypt: the pyramids line a
45-mile stretch to the west of the Nile Valley.

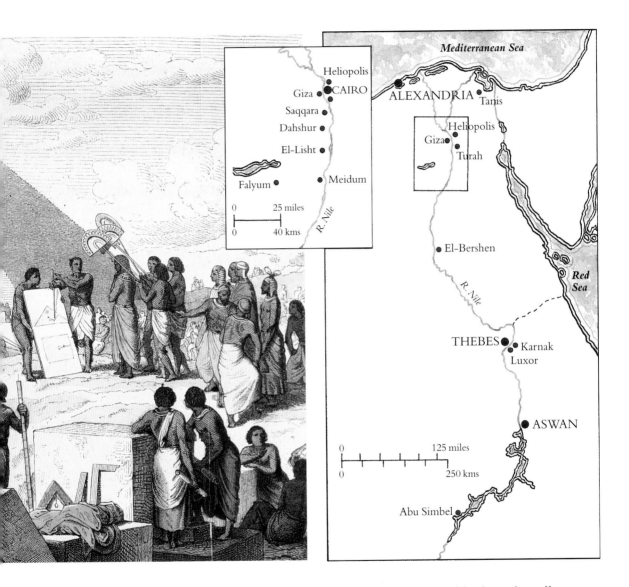

The builders composed the bulk of the pyramid from roughly shaped small stones set in a mortar of desert clay called *tafla*. They inclined the horizontal courses towards the core of the pyramid to form a series of accretions that lean inwards, like the multiple layers of an onion, one against the other. Never having attempted such heights with mudbrick, wood, or reed, the builders were worried about stability and must have seen their inward-leaning accretions as a solution.

They added an outer shell of finer limestone from quarries across the Nile valley around Turah.

Not long after Djoser, the period of colossal pyramids began. Sneferu, the first king of Dynasty 4, completed the next large pyramid at Meidum, about 37 miles south of Giza. Today the Meidum pyramid is a truncated stone tower, stripped of its outer mantle. As a result, we can see that Sneferu started with a seven-step pyramid, but enlarged it almost immediately to eight steps. His builders still used courses of relatively small blocks set in *tafla* mortar, like the Djoser Step Pyramid. At Meidum they established the standard arrangement of a royal pyramid tomb. From near the centre of the north face a long passage slopes down to the burial chamber at the very core of the pyramid. Unsure about the advisability of piling the tonnage of the pyramid on to a ceiling, the builders roofed the chamber by jutting the upper masonry courses of the walls in until they met – a technique called corbelling.

For reasons unknown, around the fifteenth year of his rule Sneferu abandoned Meidum to begin an entirely new pyramid at Dahshur just south of Saqqara. This first true pyramid was intended to have smooth faces that sloped a steep 60°. The builders used larger blocks, but tilted them toward the centre of the pyramid. As at Meidum they built upon the desert gravel and clay, but here at Dahshur the softer surface soon caused the great mass to settle unevenly. To guard against collapse they added a girdle of large stones around the base of the pyramid, reducing its slope to 54° 31' 13". They then went on to build upwards, hoping to exceed the height of Djoser's pyramid which rose within view some 13 miles to the north. But severe fissures that show to this day rent both core and casing, robbing the builders of their confidence. They realized that their inclined beds of masonry did not increase stability, so at about half the height of the pyramid they began to use horizontal courses and reduced the angle to 43° 21', creating the Bent Pyramid.

Motivated, perhaps, by the inauspiciousness of a cracking pyramid, the king ordered his builders to begin yet a third. Situated several hundred metres north of the Bent Pyramid, this new one was a comfortable 43° from the start. During his last years, as he finished both the top of the Bent Pyramid and the northern

BELOW LEFT The early Step Pyramid. BELOW RIGHT The Meidum pyramid
where the standard arrangement of royal tombs was established.
BOTTOM The interior of Meidum showing the long, downward shaft to
the burial chamber.

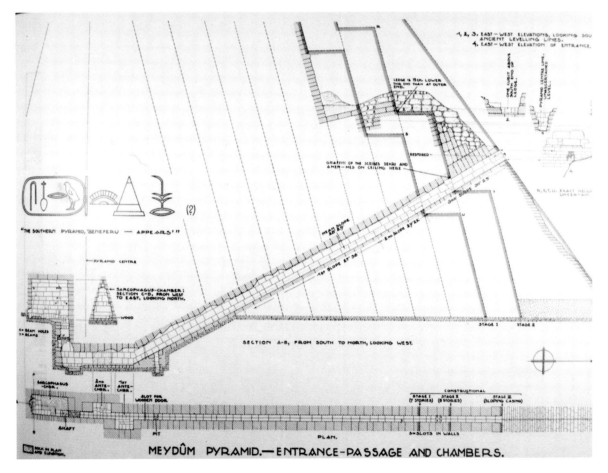

MEYDÛM PYRAMID.—ENTRANCE-PASSAGE AND CHAMBERS.

The Bent Pyramid at Dahshur, south of Saqqara.

Dahshur Pyramid, Sneferu sent another work crew back to Meidum to transform his old Step Pyramid into a true pyramid of 51° 50' 35", practically the same as the Great Pyramid of his son Khufu. In simple form, Sneferu added to the Meidum Pyramid the elements that would come to make up the standard pyramid complex: a small mortuary temple, causeway and a valley temple, or here, perhaps, a simple quay.

This arrangement and the 52° slope set the pattern for the Great Pyramid of Khufu at Giza, followed by the pyramid of his son Khafre which was nearly equal in size at a slope of 53°. The much smaller Giza pyramid of Menkaure ended the short series of five gigantic stone-block pyramids, built within three generations in Dynasty 4. The kings of Dynasties 5 and 6 abandoned large stone blocks, opting for a standardized core of more irregular and smaller stones and a great deal of loose fill. When these pyramids were robbed of their fine casing, they slumped into heaps of rubble. Building these and the Middle Kingdom pyramids of mudbrick were very different tasks from building the gigantic stone pyramids of Dynasty 4.

BELOW The Great Pyramid of Khufu with surrounding *mastabas*; view from the south-east looking north-west. BOTTOM Plan of Giza.

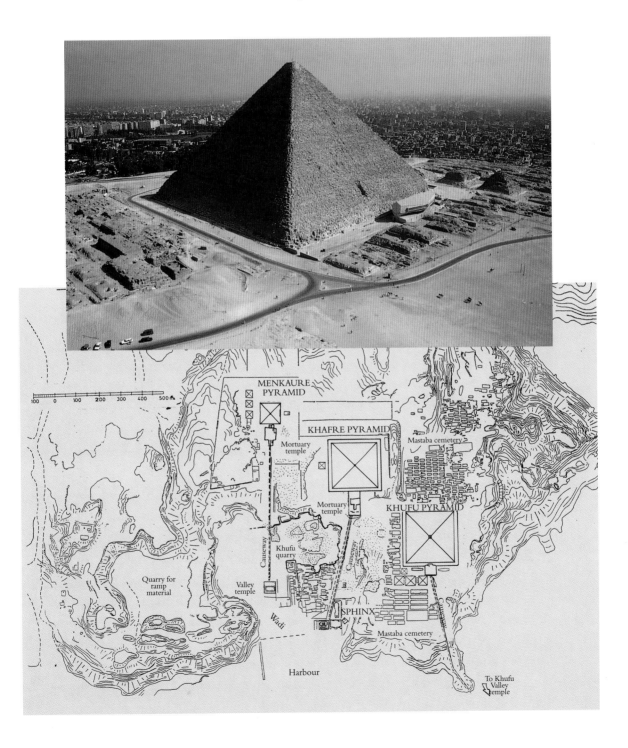

SELECTING A SITE

In the classic complex the pyramid had to be close to the valley floor, where it could be reached by a canal, yet far enough out in the desert to achieve the dramatic effect of approaching it via a long causeway. Ideally, the site would be fairly flat. Our team had different considerations. Building on the Giza Plateau, a protected antiquities zone, was out of the question. We had to settle for land generously donated by the Mena House Hotel, at the northern foot of the plateau, down-slope and down-wind from the kitchen. Although this did not match the ancient pyramid setting, the Great Pyramid of Khufu loomed behind us to the south-east and the smell of French fries told us when it was time for lunch and dinner.

Khufu's planners needed a source – preferably close by – for the enormous quantity of core stone that would form the bulk of the pyramid. In addition, they needed material to make ramps, roadways and embankments that would be comparable in volume to that of the pyramid itself. A workforce of thousands needed to be housed and fed close to the construction site. Although the bulk of the material for the pyramid could be quarried near the site, thousands of tonnes of fine Turah limestone had to be brought from the opposite side of the valley. Huge granite beams would come from Aswan, 500 miles to the south. Also transported to the foot of the plateau were unskilled workers employed on a rotating basis; gypsum and basalt from the Fayum; copper from Sinai; and wood for levers, sleds and track as well as wood fuel for cooking, preparing gypsum mortar and making copper tools. These deliveries required a substantial harbour with quays for unloading, space for barges to turn around, and nearby storage and production facilities. Giza proved to be an excellent location for this infrastructure.

Along the high north-west side of the plateau a hard embankment of stone composed of nummulites, coin-shaped fossil shells of an extinct organism, formed a perfect foundation that would not give rise to the problems that Sneferu's builders had encountered when building on the desert clays and gravel. The low south-east side of the Giza Plateau is composed of thick limestone layers that alternate soft-hard-soft-hard – just right for extracting large blocks for

The site at the northern foot of the Giza Plateau where the
construction of our pyramid began.

the core of the pyramid. Khufu's builders opened a quarry 300 metres due south
of the pyramid site that exploited this ideal layering. Further south rises another
formation with thin crumbly layers of clay and limestone. Here they quarried
material to build ramps. The broad wadi (a dry watercourse) between the two
plateaus would serve as a conduit for delivering granite, casing stone and gypsum
from outside Giza. The natural depression at the opening of the wadi may already
have retained water after each annual Nile flood, and served very well as a
harbour. The wadi led to the mouth of the quarry, from which materials flowed
up the construction ramps to be placed within the pyramid.

SELECTING A CREW

Skilled builders and craftsmen no doubt worked for the Pharaoh on a permanent basis. Peasant farmers were organized into competing gangs whose names were compounded with that of the reigning king, such as 'Friends of Khufu' or 'Drunkards of Menkaure'. Each gang was further divided into five phyles (the Greek word for 'tribe') which had the same name in each gang: the Great (or Starboard), the Asiatic (or Port), the Green (or Prow), the Little (or Stern) and the Good (or Last) Phyle. Ten to twenty men composed the smallest labour units, the divisions of a phyle. Divisions were named with single hieroglyphs for ideas such as 'life', 'endurance' and 'perfection'.

Much less dramatically, in the late twentieth century we hired rather than conscripted. Reis ('Overseer') Abd al-Wahab led thirty men who had excavated with me at Giza for fifteen years and who now provided unskilled labour. Quarry master Ahmed led fourteen skilled Egyptian masons on the building site and twelve men in the distant quarry that had been newly opened about the time we started our pyramid.

HAULING THE BLOCKS OF STONE

Roger and I found ourselves in a stone construction yard with a crew of forty-four and three weeks to assemble 186 stones into a small pyramid, measuring 9 metres at the base and 6 metres high – a pyramid that would fit nicely on the truncated top of the Great Pyramid looming on the horizon behind us. The blocks weighed from three-quarters of a tonne to three tonnes. To sort these out and to clear a space for the pyramid we first needed rope, but both the quarry-men and the villagers rejected out of hand our first consignment of 2.5-cm-thick rope, saying that it was too dry and therefore lacked tensile strength. When first used on a large block it snapped straightaway. Ahmed then ordered rope of 4 cm diameter treated with oil. This rope was sufficiently thin for the men to get a good grip, yet strong enough to be used when tumbling blocks.

The time-consuming method of tumbling the stone blocks and
the more efficient way of hauling the weight after loading it on a
wooden sled.

For tumbling, the men put a rope lasso, or a sling of synthetic material that Roger Hopkins brought, around the top of a 2- or 3-tonne block. As few as thirteen men pulled on a single or double length of rope while four men pushed from behind and two men prised up the back of the block with levers. One tug lifted the back end of the block enough to get purchase with the levers. Before the block could pivot on its lower front edge and fall over, the experienced quarrymen usually put a smaller stone on the ground in front of the block to act as a fulcrum so that it could be pivoted again easily. Until it arrives at its final destination, 'flat bedding' a very heavy load is never desirable.

But tumbling took time, and it would have been difficult to roll all the blocks up the incline of the ramp quickly enough to build the pyramid within the king's lifetime. Unlike the Incas, as will be seen in Chapter 5, the Ancient Egyptians moved heavy weights on wooden sleds as shown in relief-carved pictures on the walls of tomb and temples. When our custom-made and not inexpensive replicas of ancient wooden sleds arrived at the site, our team put one on the track and tumbled a 4.5-tonne block next to it, hoping that a final roll would mount the block on to the sled. The block hit the sled off-centre, pushing one runner into the soft sand and chewing the edge to splinters. Pinched between block and ground, the sled stuck up in the air at a 30° angle, much to everyone's frustration. After several more attempts the men became more adept at loading a multi-tonne block on a much lighter wooden sled – the first of many lessons which demostrated that long experience was one of the primary ingredients in the best ancient technology.

In order to use small cylindrical pieces of hard wood as rollers, the bottom surface of the load (or the sled that carries it) and the top surface of the road must be hard and smooth. But unless a crew possesses a gargantuan supply of wooden rollers (which would themselves have been labour-intensive to produce in a country short on trees and lacking the modern lathe), each roller must be taken from behind the load after it has passed, brought to the front and carefully replaced in front of the runners of the sled.

We found that as few as ten men on two lines could pull a 2-tonne block up a gradient that matched the lower parts of the pyramid construction ramps.

With the load advancing at a fair speed, a man must rapidly take each roller from those collecting at the rear, and place it upon the track exactly perpendicular to the direction of the load. If he turns the rollers even slightly to one side of the track, the load follows and is likely to become stuck. In the upper reaches of the pyramid, any departure from the track could have led to the loss of the block and possibly to the injury or death of the crews working below. Also, if the worker placing the rollers in front of the load lost his concentration or was not synchronized with the pullers, the load could easily roll over and crush his hand.

We found it particularly awkward to keep the load on a track of parallel wooden planks laid over the soft sand. We also tried rollers on the much broader paved road that rises toward the Giza Plateau behind the Mena House Hotel, and here the operation went much better. It was certainly within the Ancient Egyptians' ability to make hard-bed roadways.

To manoeuvre heavy loads the Egyptians also used round balls of a hard black stone called dolerite. These started out as heavy, pear-shaped hammerstones that the ancient masons used two-handed to shape hard rock such as granite, continually turning the hammerstones to strike along an edge until the entire stone was rounded. Archaeologists have found dolerite balls underneath heavy stone coffins in tombs at Giza; the workmen used them as pivots and rollers to position the sarcophagus in the tight confines of the subterranean chambers. One or two of our workmen could pivot a 2-tonne block on a hard round cobblestone.

Wall paintings in Egyptian tombs show lines of men on ropes dragging statues of the tomb owner on a sled. A man pours water from a jar on to the surface just in front of the runners of the sled. In the tomb of the 12th Dynasty nobleman Djehuty-hotep, at the site of el-Bersheh, his colossal statue, estimated to have weighed 58 tonnes, is shown being dragged in this fashion from the alabaster quarries.

At Lisht, near the 12th Dynasty pyramids of Amenemhet I and Senwosret I, archaeologists have found hauling tracks composed of a bed of limestone chips and mortar, upon which the ancient workmen embedded wooden beams that

An illustration of the wall painting in the tomb of Djehuty-hotep
shows his colossal statue being moved by a team of men dragging it
on a wooden sled.

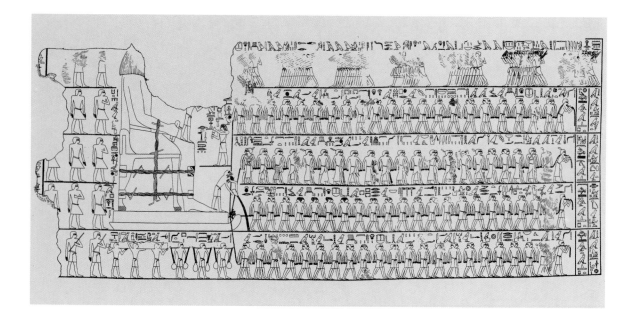

were once parts of ships' hulls. The pieces of wood are regularly spaced like railway sleepers. Thin layers of both alluvial mud from the Nile valley and white
gypsum, that must have been deposited as a lubricating liquid, run slightly above
the top surface of the beams.

Following these ancient specifications we built a track using the tan-
coloured desert clay called *tafla*. We used rollers to bring a block loaded on a sled
to the beginning of the track. As one of our workmen began to sprinkle water
just ahead of the sled, everyone, including the experienced quarrymen, protested
loudly at the very idea of dragging the load down the track on lubricated clay.
But at the first attempt the load slid along with ease. Twelve to twenty men could
pull a 2-tonne block! With the wooden planks providing a firm base, the sled
runners did not get bogged down in the *tafla*. The fact that the ends of the
runners turn up also helps prevent the sled getting stuck. In spite of the success of
this experiment Roger used the front-end loader to speed up the work so that,
before we reached the end of our tight production schedule, we could try out
various techniques that might have been used thousands of years ago in the
higher parts of the pyramid.

The hauling track for our wooden sled was built by using
tafla clay and pieces of wood laid like railway sleepers.

LAYING OUT THE PYRAMID BASE

The pyramid builders started with a square on the ground that they managed to orient to the cardinal directions with amazing accuracy. Preparing the pyramid baseline involved three separate tasks: finding true north to orient the pyramid, drawing a true square and levelling. When they built pyramids directly on the natural desert surface the ancient surveyors only needed to perform these operations once. As soon as they had the square of the base, the builders could receive the first trains of stone-laden sleds and start setting the blocks.

Things were not so simple for Khufu and Khafre's builders, because they started at Giza with a sloping surface of natural stone. They carved away the higher western corners to the level they chose for the base. For the Khafre Pyramid they simultaneously built up the opposite eastern corners. As they cut down, they left an irregular patch of natural rock protruding as high as 7 metres in the middle of the square. The builders only levelled an area about the width of a city street around the base of this core, and then only approximately. In fact their best levelling in bedrock was about as wide as a modern pavement. The masons did their finest levelling of the Khufu Pyramid – off by only 2.1 cm in the entire circumference – on a platform built of fine limestone slabs. The baseline of the Khafre Pyramid was simply a vertical cut in the foot of the bottom casing course of granite, where the slope of the pyramid would meet the top surface of the pavement of the pyramid court. The layout and levelling of these pyramids therefore presents a 'chicken and egg' situation. In order to know where to level approximately, the builders had to lay out the square. But for the accuracy of the square with the mass of natural rock protruding in the centre, they needed a surface that was as level as possible.

The builders responded to this paradox with a method of successive approximation, first drawing their lines on the sloping natural surface 7–10 metres higher than the eventual level of the pyramid base. They then projected their lines down in lead trenches as they worked the surface away. At various stages they refined their orientation to the cardinal directions and the perpendicularity of their corners. As they quarried away the rock to the level of the final baseline, the rough cube of natural rock that they left in the middle of the square prevented them from measuring the diagonals from one corner to another.

FINDING TRUE NORTH

Egyptologists have long suggested that the ancient surveyors determined true north by observing the circumpolar stars. Ancient texts call these stars the 'Imperishable Ones' because they neither rise nor set as they circle around the celestial pole about 26° up in the northern sky. Temple walls more than two thousand years younger than the pyramids show the king performing foundation ceremonies with Seshat and Thoth, the gods associated with writing and science. The king is 'looking at the sky, observing the stars, and turning his gaze toward the Great Bear'. The king and Seshat pound long stakes connected by a looping cord.

In his book *The Pyramids,* I. E. S. Edwards suggests that the ancient surveyors could have constructed a circular wall 'with a diameter of a few feet on the already levelled rock-bed of the pyramid'. Standing in the centre of the circle and facing north, the observer could mark the point at which a star rose above the wall on his right (east) and where it set below the wall on his left (west). Bisecting the angle between rising and setting points (plumbed down to the base of the wall) and the centre of the circle would give true north. In the darkness of night the ancient surveyors would have needed candles or oil lamps to illuminate the points along the wall. They would also have had to extend the resulting north line, only half of 'a few feet', more than 230 metres (755 feet). The slightest inaccuracy, even a fraction of a millimetre, in the original north line would have vastly increased, in what surveyors call 'the angle of error', the further this line was extended.

The same scenes and texts of cord-stretching ceremonies also speak of 'the shadow' and the 'stride of Ra', hinting perhaps that the Egyptian surveyors used sun and shadow in an old Boy Scout technique to find true north. This idea was developed by Martin Isler, graphic designer, sculptor and avid theorist who has written a number of articles on pyramid building in scholarly journals, and who joined our team in Egypt. The method is based on the awareness that the sun rises and sets in equal and opposite angles to the meridian (true north). A tall pole, or gnomon, is plumbed to vertical. The length of its shadow on a level surface is measured about two to three hours before noon. This becomes the radius of a circle that is inscribed with a cord and stick with the pole as its centre. As the sun rises in the sky toward noon, the shadow withdraws from the circle. In the afternoon the shadow lengthens again, forming an angle with the line of the morning shadow. When its end touches the circle again, the bisection of the angle between morning and afternoon corresponds to the meridian. The method is most accurate if carried out during the solstices.

Martin demonstrated his method for us using miniature models. Roger then carried out the same operation with a straight rod set in the ground about 2 metres from the east side of the square that we had already approximated for the base of the pyramid. His gnomon was 1.38 metres high. The radius of his circle, given by the shadow three hours before noon, was 1.77 metres. The line between the morning and afternoon points where the tip of the gnomon shadow touched the circle measured 2.9 metres. This was halved to make 1.45 metres, and the perpendicular line from the pole to the half-mark was our north line.

EXTENDING AND MEASURING THE LINE

After finding true north the ancient surveyors had to carry out several more operations in order to lay out the pyramid base. First, they had to extend their north line of a few metres, derived from stars or shadows, for a length of more than two football pitches without deviating east or west. Second, along this extended line they had to measure the distance of one side of the pyramid base. Third, they had to turn good right-angles at the corners. Finally they had to repeat these operations to measure the perpendicular sides to the opposite corners and turn another set of right-angles.

Using a method thought to have been employed by Egyptian surveyors, Roger experiments with a gnomon to find true north.

The suggestions for how the Egyptians found north all assume an initial starting point – the centre of the circle in both Edwards' north star and Isler's sun/shadow method – and result in a very short north line. How can the line be extended while keeping the north orientation? Using the shadow method, Roger and I experimented with a series of gnomons, arrayed roughly north to south but staggered slightly east to west. These gave us series of short parallel north lines, staggered along the east side of our pyramid base. We could use each short north line as an orientation check as we extended the main reference line for the pyramid base.

Extending the line over great distances probably involved pounding stakes into the ground, as the king and the goddess Seshat do in scenes of founding temples on fragments of relief from a sun temple of the 5th Dynasty king Niuserre, and again on temple walls from the Greco-Roman period. Setting stakes was easy enough on the valley floor or around pyramids built on the desert clays and gravel, but the final layout of the Khufu and Khafre Pyramids was on prepared limestone bedrock. The bottom casing blocks of both weighed many tonnes, and it is probable that the builders would have scraped, scratched, pounded and buried the setting line as they began to build the bottom of the pyramid. They would need to check the baseline repeatedly by measuring from an outside reference line, which they might have marked with cord running across the tops of a series of stakes set in holes that run in regular lines and spacings around the bases of both pyramids.

Tomb scenes show the Egyptians measuring with cords on which increments are marked by knots; alternatively paint could have been used. But a cord would stretch and sag when measuring a distance as long as 230 metres, unless it was tied at intervals to wooden posts like the ones in which modern surveyors set nails, sometimes marking the line with string. This may, again, account for the series of regular holes along the bases of the Khufu and Khafre Pyramids. The distances between these holes are not accurate increments and do not therefore add up to an accurate measurement of length. A row of stakes allowed the surveyors to establish a taut line with cord. Once they had a good line extended a sufficient distance at the correct orientation, the ancient surveyors could have measured the length of the pyramid base in increments with rods marked in cubits, an ancient equivalent to our yard- and metre-sticks.

Having extended their north–south reference line, the next stage was to lay out a square with precise right-angles. But by the time the builders cut down the terrace of the Khufu and Khafre Pyramids and were ready to scribe the actual baseline they had already repeatedly performed the operations of extending the line and turning right-angles for the corners. They first carried out these tasks at the original surface of the plateau, some 5–10 metres higher, and kept refining the lines and angles in successive stages as they worked down. This point has been ignored by almost all pyramid-building theorists! The exactitude in the pyramid base was achieved in the same way that a sculptor creates very fine and precise surfaces on a stone statue by approaching the desired shapes very gradually in closer and closer approximations. Once again, the protrusion of natural rock left in the core of the pyramid base would have prevented the builders from measuring the diagonal to check the accuracy of their square.

At all stages, the ancient surveyors could have achieved a right-angle in one of three ways. They could have used the 'Sacred' or Pythagorean triangle – three of any unit on one side, four on the second and five on the third. Such triangles seem to be present in the design and layout of the Old Kingdom mortuary temples attached to pyramids. But the evidence is not conclusive. Alternatively they could have used the Egyptian set-square – an A-shaped tool with perpendicular legs set at right-angles and a cross-brace. One leg is placed on the already established line and the perpendicular is taken from the other leg. The square is then flipped and the operation repeated. The exact perpendicular is taken from the small angle of error between the two positions. As a third method they could have used measuring cord to pull two intersecting arcs of the same radius. A line connecting the points of intersection will be at right-angles to the original line.

Roger and I established a reference line corresponding to north along the east side of our pyramid. Two lessons were brought home the hard way, when Roger was about to set the first of the crucial corner stones. The first lesson was the need for a reference line outside the pyramid base and along all four sides. The second lesson was the advantage of building upon bedrock. To get it just right, Roger wanted to set the corner block from above by suspending it with steel cable on the scoop of the front-end loader. But the ancient builders had no such option: they had to drag the stone into place, as we insisted Roger must do. The 1.5-tonne casing block had no respect for the thin survey pin and string marking Roger's corner. When it was knocked out of place Roger lamented, 'It was much easier just to come in and set it down where it is supposed to be. I've got to re-establish that line all the way from my north–south [reference] line again in order to find this [setting] line.'

THE QUARRY

About 300 metres directly south of the Khufu Pyramid a great bite has been taken out of the slope of the plateau – a horseshoe-shaped quarry where the Egyptians had exploited the alternating thick-thin, hard-soft sequence of layers. Cut into the western wall of the quarry are a series of 4th Dynasty tombs – three of these belong to children of Khafre, suggesting that the quarry was no longer used in his reign. This must be the quarry that furnished the bulk of the core stone for Khufu's Great Pyramid. Although that western edge always showed above the surface, in the previous century the quarry was filled with millions of cubic metres of limestone chips, gypsum, sand and *tafla* – probably the remains of the ramp that the workers pushed back into the quarry as they completed the pyramid.

In the 1920s and 1930s the Egyptian archaeologist Selim Hassan carted away much of this debris. Where he cleared the bottom one can still see rock shelves, about 1.5 metres high, that the quarrymen left when they separated blocks the size of those in the core of the pyramid. I stood at the bottom of the quarry with Nick Fairplay, an English master carver who has visited many quarries from Italy to Indiana and can see the living hand of ancient masons and craftsmen when he looks at mute stone blocks and tool marks. Nick was shocked at the depth of the quarry – some 30 metres. Given its breadth of just over 230 metres, the volume of missing stone is about 2 700 000 metres^3, comparable to the 2 650 000 metres^3 in Khufu's Great Pyramid.

On the surface behind the rock shelf there are long narrow channels that the ancient quarrymen cut to define the width of the blocks they would take away. Ahmed's quarrymen made similar banks and channels to separate the blocks for our own pyramid. Their quarry to the south-east of Cairo, on the opposite bank of the River Nile from Giza, yields fine-grained homogeneous white limestone similar to the Turah stone which was used for the ancient pyramid casings. It amazed us that only twelve men, working withnothing on their feet and sleeping in a lean-to against the rock walls, quarried 186 stones in twenty-two days for our pyramid.

It took Ahmed's team of twelve quarrymen only twenty-two days to
cut the 186 blocks of white limestone needed to build our pyramid.

Perhaps the hardest work was cutting the channels to define the banks of
rock that were, in turn, subdivided into blocks. One man took mighty swings
with a long-handled pick, chopping out a separation trench 15–18 cm wide for
a depth, or bed height, of a little less than a metre. He deepened the trench by
extending one leg down into it, and swinging the pick directly toward his shin to
strike at the bottom of the channel. The pick man could cut about 2 metres of
channel per day. As Roger pointed out, if they wanted to separate a large block
they would have to make a wider trench, and this is what is seen on a colossal
scale in the unfinished quarries at Giza between the basin quarry directly south
of the Khufu Pyramid and the Sphinx.

Having separated the block around three sides, the ancient quarrymen
would prise it up by means of wooden levers which were as thick as railway

sleepers. Ahmed's quarrymen were practising a more evolved form of this principle, made possible by the development of iron (as opposed to wood, stone, and copper) tools. In place of yawning sockets for wooden levers they used iron wedges, shims and feathers, hammered into slots that only needed to be 7–8 cm high, 38 cm long and 14 cm deep. A series of such wedges would split the block from its bed.

Again and again in our experiments we found this advantage of iron tools over those of the ancient pyramid builders: iron and steel deliver more force to a significantly smaller area. Another example was the way Ahmed's workmen made use of iron crowbars. The best stone setter of his crew was an eighteen-year-old named Adel, not because he was stronger than all the rest (in fact he was thin and slight of build) but because he could make a 2-tonne block dance through the skilful use of his crowbar and small pivoting manoeuvres. Adel's skills would not have worked with a copper rod, which would simply have given way to the stone and bent. And a wooden lever needs to be much thicker, as seen in the ancient lever sockets.

More quarrymen worked across the Nile valley at Turah to get the fine white limestone for the outer casing. Here they cut deep galleries into the escarpment to follow the best layers of stone, beginning with a 'lead' shelf that would become the ceiling of the gallery. They took the stone along terraces or banks, as they did in the bottom of the Giza quarry. The granite quarries were 500 miles to the south at Aswan, where Khufu employed men to extract the enormous blocks for lining his burial chamber and for plugging his pyramid passage; Khafre and Menkaure used even more granite. The Pharaoh's navy floated the granite down the Nile on large barges that have so far remained lost to archaeologists.

STONE CUTTING

Ahmed's masons made short work of cutting limestone with their iron tools such as the *shahoota,* a heavy hammer that thins to a razor-sharp line of teeth at both ends. The hammer-wielder grips the tool just below the head and strikes the stone rhythmically at an acute angle, shaving the surface with great accuracy. The fine teeth that leave a combed signature in modern masonry would be destroyed in the first few blows of a similarly shaped hammer made of copper.

Alongside these post-Iron Age advances, our men used masonry techniques that have remained the same since the time of the pyramids. For example, they split very large blocks by simply etching a line with the corner of a heavy flat-headed hammer, then pounding the surface directly until the stone fell apart at the desired place. Intuition and the sound of their blows tell them just when and where the stone will split. Modern masons use the flat end of smaller hammers to dress the surface of a block by hitting it directly, which causes thin slivers to flake off the surface. Ancient masons did the same, albeit with hammers of stone.

Copper chisels will cut limestone, as we demonstrated on our pyramid, but the ancient masons must have sharpened and reworked their tools far more often than their modern counterparts. Nick Fairplay estimates that they would have needed one full-time tool sharpener per every hundred stone cutters. The chisels used for fine dressing were all the width of a thumb or less, as evidenced by the marks that the masons did not sand away. The ancient masons also made ample use of a metal point, or 'nail', to work limestone. Like masons and sculptors of all time and places, they used the point to rough out the desired form in stone. The evidence can be seen in the long, thin, deep strokes on the walls of tomb shafts and in unfinished jobs such as the Subterranean Chamber of Khufu's Pyramid.

The Egyptians of the Pyramid Age also sawed and drilled very hard stone. Numerous saw marks can still be seen on the sides and bases of the black basalt slabs of the Khufu Mortuary Temple. Sir William Matthew Flinders Petrie, the British archaeologist who made the first scientific survey of the Great Pyramid, observed the saw marks on the red granite sarcophagus in the King's Chamber. How can soft copper tools saw and drill such extremely hard stone? Probably with the assistance of quartz sand in a wet slurry – the quartz does the cutting, while the metal tools simply guide the abrasive mixture. Some of the cuts in the basalt of the Khufu Mortuary Temple still retain a dried mixture of quartz sand and gypsum tinted green from the copper blade.

OPPOSITE, ABOVE LEFT The puzzle of ramp construction:(a) an impractical, too steep slope; (b) a practical 1 in 10 slope, but an extremely long length; (c) the probable solution – a wrap-around ramp.

RAMPS

There are only three basic techniques that the Ancient Egyptians could have used for lifting blocks: the inclined plane or ramp, levering, and some assembly using rope, wood and stone. To raise most of the stone the builders probably used ramps that, however shaped, must have been enormous structures in their own right. We should expect to find massive deposits of the material from which they were composed. Many books about the pyramids suggest that the ramps were made of mudbrick, and archaeologists have found mudbrick ramps near the Middle Kingdom pyramids of Lisht. At Giza, there are no great deposits of mud rubble from which to construct the necessary gigantic ramp. The quarries to the south of the pyramids are filled instead with millions of cubic metres of *tafla,* gypsum and limestone chips. This must be the material left over from the pyramid ramps, but could the builders have used it to make an ascent against the ever-narrowing faces of the pyramid more than 100 metres up in the air?

The form of the construction ramps is a persistent puzzle. There are two main possibilities: a sloping, straight ramp that ascends one face of the pyramid, and one or more ramps that begin near the base and wrap around the pyramid as it rises.

The problem with the straight-on ramp is that it must be lengthened each time its height against the pyramid is increased in order to maintain a slope of no more than one unit of rise in ten units of length. Either work stops at such times, or the ramp is built in two sections and one side is used by the builders while the ramp crew raises and lengthens the other half. The ramp would need to be ex-tremely long in order to maintain a usable slope up to the highest part of the pyramid. At Giza, the ramp for the Great Pyramid would have had to go far to the south, well beyond the quarry where Khufu's builders took most of the stone for the core of his pyramid.

The wrap-around ramp was probably supported either on the slope of the pyramid or on the ground and leaning against its faces like a giant envelope with a rising roadbed on top. Since the latter cloaks the entire edifice, as the pyramid rises it would be difficult to control squareness and slope by checking back to the

BELOW RIGHT The unfinished granite casing on the lower
part of the Menkaure Pyramid.
BOTTOM Our ramp to the top of the first course of the pyramid.

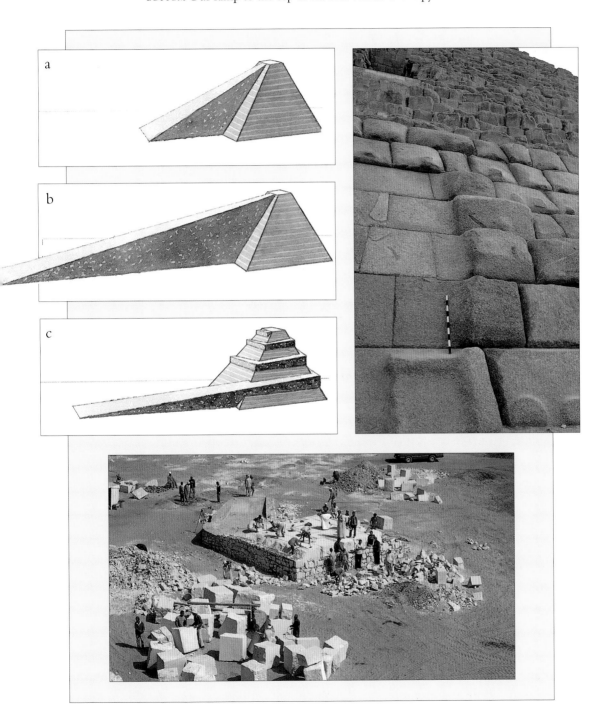

part already built. If the ramp is actually founded on the 52–53° sloping faces, enough extra stone must be left on the casing blocks in steps wide enough to support the ramp. The granite casing on the lower part of the Menkaure Pyramid at Giza is unfinished, but the extra stock of stone does not seem adequate to support a roadway on the 52° slope. Both kinds of spiral ramp run into trouble near the top of the pyramid, where the slope becomes increasingly steep and the faces of the pyramid too narrow to support a ramp from one corner to the next.

Near the base of the pyramid, the builders could have delivered stone over many short ramps. At higher levels, they needed some rise in the run of the ramp from the quarry to the pyramid. Since we know the location of the quarry that probably served the Khufu Pyramid, we also know that if the ramp began at the north mouth of the quarry it would have extended 320 metres to the south-west base of the pyramid. If it rose 30 metres above the base, it would have sloped 6° 36'. At this height nearly 50 per cent of the pyramid was already in place. The Khufu roadbed could have climbed up and around the pyramid, its slope increasing against each face, reaching a height of 95 metres above the pyramid, two-thirds the total height when nearly nearly 96 per cent of the pyramid was complete. However, three sides of the pyramid trunk would already have been enveloped by the supporting embankments, and the fourth would have to be covered to make the rest of the ascent at intolerably steep angles.

Knowing that we did not have the solution to the troubles at the top, our ramp consisted of retaining walls of *tafla,* limestone chips and gypsum, about 60 cm thick. The ramp approached the top of the north-west corner of the first course of our pyramid for a rise of 1 metre in 14 metres length. We set wooden sleepers every 90 cm. The second section ran 10.34 metres along the west face for a rise of 73 cm and had a width of 2.9 metres. Here our ramp turned a corner to run along the unfinished south face of our pyramid for a width of 2.7 metres. We were surprised that a small crew of builders who specialize in clay and broken stone completed all this in less than three days.

Next they extended the ramp along the south face of our pyramid, the roadbed rising towards the south-east corner with the foundation on the ground. When we came to the fourth (north-east) corner of the pyramid we were faced with a decision: should we build a foundation for the roadbed all the way down to the pyramid base and in so doing mask its north face, or should we try to base the roadbed on the slope of the pyramid itself? Roger opted for the second possibility, but he used casing blocks with considerable extra stock of stone to form a ledge on which he supported the retaining walls of the ramp. Alas, he did not have time to do more than the corner stone in this fashion.

If the ancient builders had opted for this solution, it would have been necessary to leave protruding casing stones staggered diagonally across the pyramid face in order to allow the ramp to rise, or else horizontal courses could have protruded at certain intervals so that the base of the retaining wall of the ramp would be level but step up at intervals, while the roadbed rose at a gradient. Recently, Zahi Hawass has excavated the bases of Khufu's Queens' Pyramids to reveal that a great deal of extra stock was left, stepped one course down to another, on undressed bottom courses of casing stone. These may be unusual because they are part of the foundation, but if this much extra stock was left on all the casing stones it might well have supported a spiral ramp like the one that Roger started. He calculated that a spiral ramp would have wrapped around the Khufu Pyramid five times to reach the top.

Twenty men could pull a 1-tonne block up the incline. For turning the direction of pull at the corner, Roger embedded two stout wooden posts deep into a thickening of the ramp's retaining wall to keep them firm against the pressure the pullers would exert. Each post was 20 cm in diameter, spaced 85 cm apart. Instead of wooden sleepers, Roger embedded into the roadbed a slab of limestone which would give a hard surface to turn the load by levering. When the pullers reached the corner Roger adjusted the ropes around the posts, which he lubricated to reduce friction. Some men pulled from around the corner, others pulled down the slope with the ropes reversing direction around the posts. At the corner, the men easily levered the load to its new orientation.

The ancient workmen needed to remove the ramps as they finished the pyramid. Using picks, our men easily broke down our ramp into its constituent limestone chips, gypsum and clay. Deconstructing a gigantic ramp of dense mud-brick might have been more difficult.

Martin Isler's method of leverage was tested on the south side
of our pyramid.

LEVERING

Some pyramid theorists say that no matter how a ramp is designed it requires too much material – rivalling the bulk of the pyramid – to have been practical. They suggest that many of the stones were raised by levering even though ancient evidence indicates that this technique was mostly used for side movements and final adjustments.

It is true that levers can be used for see-sawing a block upwards by raising one side at a time and placing supports underneath, then raising and supporting the opposite side. But to anyone who manages to climb the Khufu or Khafre pyramids one thing becomes clear: it is inconceivable that such lever-lifting took place on the stepped courses of the core stone or the undressed casing stone. Those who think so have in mind very regular wide courses, like those of a stairway. But here the courses are less regular, and at a metre or less in width, there is not enough space for teams of men to lever up blocks weighing 1 tonne or more. Without a working platform, the sheer slope of the pyramid precludes levering many tonnes of stone for the higher courses.

Martin Isler proposed such working platforms and, in place of ramps, stairways on which the pyramid builders levered up the stone to build the upper parts of the pyramids. He illustrates his theory with drawings of massive mudbrick stairways against the centre of each pyramid face, making them look like Mayan pyramids. Hundreds of workmen lever stone blocks up these steps and onto working platforms that are founded, like Roger's spiral ramp, on extra stock of stone left on the casing blocks. The builders rocked the stones up and tumbled them over on to each step of the supply stairway.

Isler agreed to test his method with a 680-kg stone on the unfinished south side of our pyramid. Two levers and four men were used on each side of the block. Two additional men worked in front of the block, inserting supports.

Each pull of the levers raised the side of the block just enough to slip in an industrially planed flat board. Immediately a question arises: using this technique, how much flat-planed wood would have been required to build the Khufu Pyramid? The amount of wood used for levers and sleds alone must have been enormous, but it would have vastly increased if the builders raised all the blocks on wooden supports. The fact that the supports must be planed smooth also vastly increases the amount of work. If the supports are not planed smooth, the stack becomes unstable as it rises. Even with our machine-planed boards the support stack, comprising twelve layers of board for a 72-cm rise, became unwieldy, as did the lever fulcrums. In order to get purchase the fulcrum – a tottering stack of stone – had to be raised as the block went up. In spite of these worries, after a very tense two hours our men had raised the block 86 cm.

So the levering worked, but it is doubtful that the Egyptians raised most of the stones in this way. It is very possible, however, that levering was the only means to raise the blocks of the highest courses, near the apex, once the builders had brought them as far as they could on ramps.

INSIDE KHUFU'S GREAT PYRAMID AT GIZA

The ancient workmen left the Subterranean Chamber, some 30 metres below the pyramid base, half hewn out of the bedrock. Perhaps the king changed his mind about the location of his burial chamber; alternatively if all three chambers in the pyramid were a unified design from the beginning, this one might have been given up because it was so difficult to complete at the end of the Descending Passage, a 105-metre stone tube slightly more than a metre in height and width, sloping up about 26° towards the circumpolar stars, the 'Imperishable Ones' that neither rise nor set, an image of eternity and a destination of the king in the afterlife.

The work in the chamber was far from pleasant. Chips flew from the stonework. Dust from hauling the waste up and out of the passage filled the air. Oil lamps or slow-burning torches provided the only light. But the human suffering involved in making the chamber in the bowels of the bedrock was inconsequential compared to the need to aim Khufu's spirit to the Imperishable stars. No other king put a pyramid chamber so deep in the earth at the end of such a long, narrow passage.

North–south cross-section of the Khufu Pyramid. The thin 'air
channels' leading from the King's and Queen's Chambers are conduits
for the king's soul to ascend to the stars.

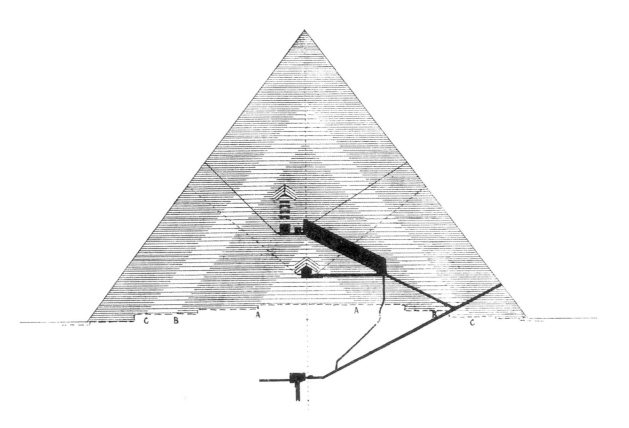

Khufu also stretched the engineering capabilities of his time to put a
chamber higher in the pyramid than any other king before or after. The
Ascending Passage slopes up 26° from the Descending Passage into the pyramid
for a distance of 39 metres and is a little more than 1 metre square. Suddenly the
chute rises to a height of 8.5 metres, continuing its sweep up into the pyramid.
The sides of this Grand Gallery are corbelled inward until they meet at a ceiling
1.05 metres wide. This is the same width as the floor passage which runs between
two side ramps, each with a series of deep notches for wooden beams to hold
back the granite plugging blocks. After the king's funeral the granite plugs would
slide down the centre passage and straight into the Ascending Passage.

From the bottom of the Grand Gallery the Horizontal Passage leads to the misnamed 'Queen's Chamber'. Here for the first time the builders used huge gabled limestone beams like an inverted 'V' to form a roof, so that the weight of the pyramid pushes down on the low end of the beams rather than on the centre of the ceiling. A tall, corbelled niche in the east wall must have contained a statue which would make the Queen's Chamber a *serdab*, a blind stone chamber for a statue of the deceased such as those often attached to Egyptian tombs above ground.

The Grand Gallery leads to the appropriately named King's Chamber, where the priests probably put Khufu to rest in a red granite sarcophagus. Similar in form to the sarcophagus, the room is a rectangular granite box, roofed by flat beams up to 8 metres long and weighing from 40–60 tonnes. This third kind of ceiling in Khufu's Pyramid represents the first time that the builders attempted to span a distance as wide as 5.24 metres with stone laid flat. But cracks in the granite beams, filled with ancient gypsum, indicate that problems developed.

In order to lift the stresses off the King's Chamber, Khufu's engineers devised one of the most astounding features of any pyramid. They added three more granite ceilings, each spaced one course of stone, to form four stress-relieving chambers. Above these they added a fifth relieving chamber topped with pitched limestone beams like those roofing the Queen's Chamber. The first of the five chambers was entered in ancient times by way of the little crawl space from the top end of the Grand Gallery – probably to smear the gypsum in the cracks of the King's Chamber beams. The upper chambers were first entered in 1837 when the British explorer Howard Vyse blasted his way in with dynamite. On the walls of the relieving chambers he found ancient red-painted levelling lines, axis markers, and even the names of the work gangs who set the stones. The gangs compounded their names with that of the king, who is mostly here called Khnum-khuf. A beautifully preserved graffito on one of the uppermost lime-stone beams reads 'Friends of Khufu Gang'.

When the king's burial rites were finished, the workmen completed the third line of defence against robbers. They slid heavy granite portcullis slabs down three great notches in the side walls of the small antechamber leading from the top of the Grand Gallery to the King's Chamber. Next they removed the restraints on the granite blocks in the Grand Gallery, allowing the plugs to slide down into the Ascending Passage. This was the second line of defence. The last workmen to leave the pyramid escaped through a tunnel quarried from the bottom of the Grand Gallery through the already-laid masonry down to the bottom of the Descending Passage. Finally, they sealed the outer entrance with stones that matched the pyramid casing to form the first line of defence against robbery.

Ultimately, none of these mechanisms worked. Today thousands of tourists swarm into the pyramid through the robbers' tunnel that violators blasted along the pyramid's centre axis. The tunnel turns to the east to connect just above the juncture between the Ascending and Descending Passages. Legend has it that the tunnel is the work of Caliph al-Mamun in AD 820. But the violators appear to have known just how far and where to go to get to the Ascending Passage; so they might have lived within a few generations of Khufu himself, the recipients of a memory of the defence system handed down from the men who worked on the mysterious interior.

SETTING STONES

The few remaining bits of the Khufu casing are a marvel to behold. Blocks of about 7 tonnes were fitted together with joints so fine that neither knife nor razor blade can penetrate the seam. These exquisite joints run the entire length of the blocks back toward the core, in many cases more than a metre.

Roger was frustrated in his attempts to get his bottom casing stones to fit so well, in part because he built on soft sand and gravel. He had to insert small stone chips under the lower edges of his blocks to get the joint faces, which his masons precut, to come together. 'With a little practice,' Roger said, 'we could get those fine joins too.'

But he might have to change his procedure, because the ancient masons custom-cut each casing stone on the course under construction so as to achieve a perfect fit with its neighbour. They laid the casing stone on a completely flat

Remains of the bottom course of casing stone and foundation
platform on the north side of the Khufu Pyramid.

surface – either the pyramid foundation, or the top of the course just below. But
the bottom casing courses of Khufu's Queens' Pyramids and Khafre's Pyramid –
where the lowest casing is granite – are exceptions. Here the masons cut the
bedrock foundation into seats of different depths for the individual blocks so as
to bring their tops flush, forming a level surface all the way around the pyramid
at the top of the first course which must have functioned like the pavement
surface which formed the Khufu pyramid baseline.

The builders first set the corner stones and several stones in between to
establish the 'lead lines' of the four sides of the pyramid. The stone cutters had
only dressed one side which would form the bottom of each casing block. Near

their destination the blocks had to be off-loaded from the sled. The haulers might have moved the blocks the rest of the way on rollers, which would have worked well between the flat bottoms and the smooth surface below. The setting crews parked the rough corner stones above their final resting place on blocks, or on wedges placed under the rollers. The masons then cut the two side faces straight and smooth, as near as possible to the original plane of cleavage from the quarry. These faces were not necessarily at right-angles to the line of the pyramid face, or to the horizontal surface of the platform below.

At this point they could bring in the normal blocks of the first course, following the same procedures as with the corner blocks. Masons cut the joint faces of any two stones parallel by measuring from one face to another with string as they dressed the surfaces. They probably started with the corners of the joint faces and then chiselled away until they had achieved flat parallel planes. The setting crew had to park the blocks close enough for the parallel joint faces to be achieved, yet far enough apart for the masons to be able to work on the faces. The advantage of using wedges under the rollers is that the setters could remove the wedges and roll back the latest stone in order to create more room to lever the previous one into its final position.

The stone setters then lifted the corner block slightly with levers before removing the wedges and rollers to set the block on its bed. A final dressing of the joint face – probably with small chisels and sanding – left a line on the horizontal bed along the bottom corner of the joint face. (The resulting setting lines, marking the joint between blocks that are now missing, can be seen on top of preserved casing courses at the Giza Pyramids.) The first block on either side of the corner remained on supports above the bed while the setters brought the second block close to it. They trimmed the next two joint faces parallel before lowering the first regular block down on to the bed, then used levers for the final adjustment of a few centimetres, pushing the block against the joint face of the corner block. (This is why some pyramid casing blocks show lever sockets at the bottom of one joint face.) A thin film of gypsum mortar was probably used as a lubricant. The masons did a final dressing of the free joint face after they set the block down, which left another 'setting line' on the top of the course below.

MAINTAINING SLOPE AND ALIGNMENT

When they set the blocks of the pyramid casing the masons left a good amount of extra rough stone protruding on the front face of each block. There is good evidence that, by the time of the Khufu Pyramid, the practice was to shave off the extra stock of rough stone after the entire pyramid had been built, starting from the top and working down to the baseline as they removed the construction ramps and embankments. How did they know that under all the extra rough stone they had four straight corners and four good flat faces that would slope evenly to a point? How could they dress the acres of fine limestone without developing waves and modulations across the pyramid faces? The little that remains of the pyramid outer casing suggests that they trimmed the sides as accurately as if a huge blade had cut off all the extra rough stone in a single clean cut.

The answer seems to be that the masons incorporated guidelines for that cut into each and every casing block as they joined one block to another. When they set the lead casing blocks at the corners and in the middle of each side of the pyramid, the rough extra stock on the front of each block stuck out beyond the intended baseline of the pyramid. After they had dressed the sides of these blocks to be joined to the next blocks, but before they concealed the joint side by setting the next block against it, they had to draw the lines of the pyramid face – the lines along which that gigantic cut would shave away the extra stock at the end of the building project.

Measuring a set amount from an outside reference line, the masons marked the point where the baseline of the pyramid would intersect with the smoothly dressed joint sides of the block. Then they etched the slope line of the pyramid face on the joint sides. The Ancient Egyptians determined the slopes of walls with a measurement called *seqed*, the amount that the face of the wall is set back for a rise of one cubit (0.525 metres). A set back of one cubit for a rise of one cubit results in 45° slope. The nearly 52° angle of the Khufu Pyramid could be obtained from a set back, or run, of 11 to a rise of 14. Khufu's builders could measure from the already determined baseline 11 units in and 14 units up with a plumb line to mark the top of the slope. But it would have been easier to draw

Roger's masons working on their first casing course.
INSET Mark pointing out the line and bevel that guided the trimming
of the pyramid face from the extra stock of ancient casing blocks.

the slope by placing wooden set squares made to the desired angle against the joint face of each block.

Once they had marked the angle of the pyramid face on the sides of the blocks, the masons left the extra stock of stone on the outer face of each block, but bevelled it away from the lines where all four join faces (top, bottom and two sides) intersected with the plane of the pyramid face. This bevelling was a lead, created block by block, for the final dressing of the pyramid casing. When the masons bought up the next block in sequence and set it down, creating the side join with its neighbour, the new stone had extra stock on the non-joining front face, and extra dressed joint face, extending out beyond the bevelled sloping side joint of its older partner. The masons then bevelled away the extra stock on the newest block along the slope of its neighbour. Then, on the opposite free join face, they repeated the procedure, marking the slope and bevelling away the extra stock along this line and along the top and bottom where these sides intersected the sloping plane of the pyramid face.

Roger's masons did something similar in that they left extra stock of rough stone on the front face of each casing block – although not nearly as much as on the ancient stones. They also provided a kind of bevelled lead on each block for dressing down the pyramid face, but they cut their lead as a flat border around the extra stock on the front faces of the casing blocks. They did not custom trim the joint faces of match blocks, and herein lies one of the main reasons that they could not match the extraordinary fine joints of the ancients.

Block by block, the ancient masons created the sloping planes of the pyramid faces, leaving it hidden behind the extra stock of stone. If the slope as marked on one block was a little off in one direction, the others might deviate in another direction so that the errors averaged out. The last major operation was to free the pyramid faces. As the masons cut way the extra stock, the bevelled space between each block would come together. Just at the point where the spaces between adjacent blocks closed to a fine joint, the masons knew that they should not cut any deeper. They were at the desired plane of the pyramid face.

In addition to obtaining the slope by bevelling the face of the pyramid into each casing block, the builders had to avoid twist in the rising pyramid. They could have established back sights down on the ground at some distance from the pyramid base. These markers, wooden poles perhaps, would have aligned with the centre axes and diagonals of the pyramid. In fact, among the many features that have yet to be mapped in the rock floor around the large Giza Pyramids there are large holes and notches that seem to align with the major lines of the pyramids.

THE INNER STEP PYRAMID

In one sense, a pyramid is an infinite series of squares within squares, each one successively smaller and raised just the right amount to provide the desired slope of the four sides to the top point. Once the Khufu and Khafre Pyramids had risen above the mass of natural rock that the builders left in the base, the masons could measure across the square of the truncated pyramid to insure that its diagonals and sides were of equal length and thereby check its squareness. At this height the reference lines on the ground would have been inaccessible, covered with ramps and building debris. But the builders could have transferred a system of measurement and control up on to the top of the truncated pyramid. If the core masonry rose ahead of the fine outer casing, the masons could have measured out to the facial lines of the pyramid from reference points and lines on the core.

It has been suggested that every pyramid contains an inner step pyramid. Some theorists believe that the rise and run of the steps have a specific relationship to the slope of the outer casing. These ideas are inspired by the pyramid of Meidum, where the steps of the inner eight-step pyramid have fine, sharp corners and faces that could have served as references for measuring out to the slope of the enlarged true pyramid. We do not know if the largest pyramids of Dynasty 4, from Sneferu to Khafre, are built with an inner step pyramid. The partially destroyed or unfinished Queens' Pyramids of Khufu and Menkaure, and the gash in the north face of the Menkaure Pyramid, allow us to see that the core of these pyramids is composed of great rectangular blocks of crude masonry similar in form to *mastabas* – a kind of chunk-approach to assembling an inner step pyramid that lacks the beautifully finished faces and corners of Meidum. The pattern is obscured by backing stones, of almost equal size to those forming the *mastaba*-like chunks, that filled in the broad steps, and by smaller packing stones that filled the space between the core and the casing.

Built in this fashion, the core masonry must have risen a good height above the casing. The three-tiered step pyramid in the Queens' Pyramids was certainly not in itself a reference for the rise and run of the outer casing. However, the core could have carried reference lines and points with paint, pegs and cord. On the southernmost pyramid of Khufu's queens there are small holes, about 5 cm in diameter, near the corners of the tiers of the inner step pyramid. Some of these align with the sharp corners still preserved in the fine casing near the base of the pyramid. The holes might be sockets for small pegs that carried temporary cord reference lines from which the masons measured out the appropriate amount to mark the line of the outer pyramid face when the setting crews built up the casing.

GETTING TO THE POINT

Lacking evidence about the technique that the ancient builders used to raise the last blocks of the pyramid, most serious theorists assume that they used levers. The fact that any pyramid's four sides narrow towards the top means that its builders run out of room for ramps and for men to pull on ropes. Our own small pyramid was too high for Roger's favoured technique of raising stones with steel cable and the scoop of a borrowed loader. So Roger also reluctantly used levering for some last few blocks.

There was much debate on how to get the capstone to the top. Our winding ramp went two-thirds the height of our small pyramid. From there the stepped unfinished courses at the back led up to a small platform where the three finished sides awaited closure, while the fourth side of the capstone hung out over the uncased stepped courses. The masons roughed out the stone on the ground. It was small enough for the men to carry on a wooden frame, yet so

The most dangerous procedure – getting the capstone into
position at the top of the pyramid.

The result of our three-week experiment. The work which
went into our tiny effort made us look at the Great Khufu Pyramid
looming above it with even greater admiration.

heavy that, as soon as they lifted it, they realized there could be no resting or
turning back. They practically ran the load up and around the ramp. The most
dangerous moment came when the crew ascended the stepped courses to
the apex and tilted the load, which threatened to slide off and crash down the
pyramid. We wondered if for every ancient pyramid there was such a final
moment of uncertainty and tension: recently, archaeologists have discovered a
relief stone carving from the causeway of the Dynasty 5 pyramid of Sahure at
Abusir which shows dancing, singing, and celebration on setting the capstone.

THE TRIUMPH OF ANCIENT SKILLS

The body of the pyramid completed, our masons began, as did their ancient counterparts, to free, from the top down, the smooth sloping faces hidden in the rough extra stock of stone. The pyramid that our crew built in three weeks, with the assistance of modern machines, was a tiny fraction of Khufu's looming above us on the plateau beyond. But even this limited experiment made it abundantly clear that the pyramids are very human monuments, created through long experience and tremendous skill, but without any kind of secret sophistication. More than we could capture on film, our trials resulted in many insights and deep admiration for the skills of ancient builders. Everyone on our team wished that they could repeat the three-week experiment every year, for the more pyramid building we did, the better we became and the more we discovered – far more than we could hope to gain from all the theorizing in books. Where we tried the tools and techniques of the ancient builders but failed to match their best results in Khufu's Pyramid, it was due to the lack of several lifetimes of practice and not because we were missing some mysterious technology.

THE OBELISK

MICHAEL BARNES

URING the fashion for Egyptian antiquities in the nineteenth century, the classiest souvenir from the land
of the Pharaohs was an obelisk: hundreds of tonnes
of granite in one lofty, brittle needle. Moving one
to a distant land and erecting it, was tricky even with
industrial-age technology. How did the Ancient
Egyptians do it with just ropes, dirt, sticks and stones?

To confront this monumental mystery we travelled to Egypt in order to attempt
the erection of an obelisk of modest size by ancient means. We knew that before
us popes, emperors, kings, soldiers and industrialists had taken extraordinary pains
to pirate obelisks from their pedestals by the Nile and reset them in the hearts of
London, Rome, Istanbul, Paris and New York. There was even Pliny the Elder's
story that Ramses the Great had strapped one of his sons to an obelisk that was
about to be raised in order to concentrate the minds of the erection crew.
Although the slender stems are powerful forms we wondered what it was about
obelisks that drove people to such lengths.

Monoliths sacred to prehistoric societies all over the world echo the obelisk's
form. In the Egyptian creation myths, the Sea of Chaos seethed and heaved before
the world was made, a confusion of noise and substance without direction and

The head of Ramses II and his obelisk before
the temple of Luxor.

shape. The sun god Ra reached down into the chaos and drew up the first solid matter, a stone pillar called Benben; an obelisk is the refined form of Benben. In Ancient Egypt the obelisk had a dual purpose: a token of devotion to the sun god Ra, and a self-promotion for the Pharaoh. One of Ramses the Great's obelisks, now in Paris, bears a typical hieroglyphic inscription, '…a ruler great in wrath, mighty in strength, so every land trembles before him, because of his renown'.

The Pharaohs' passion for erecting enormous monolithic objects of vandal-proof hard granite, made for eternity, came to a peak during Egypt's New Kingdom (1550–1070 BC). Obelisks were usually erected in pairs at the ceremonial entrance of a temple on the occasion of a Pharaoh's jubilee or a great foreign victory. They were accompanied by a pair of sphinxes and – to associate the worldly king with the heavenly god – colossal statues of the Pharaoh. Raising obelisks aggrandized the gods and humbled men.

Our word for such structures comes from the Greek *obeliskos,* meaning a 'skewer or roasting spit'. An obelisk's four sides taper gently upwards for about seven or eight times the width of its base, and then meet a terminal pyramidion, a steeply sloped pyramid, which in ancient times was sheathed in copper, gold or electrum. The pyramidion's geometry has the same significance as the basic shapes of the great pyramids: their planes draw together all four directions and raise them toward heaven; they also imply that all form and all directions emanate downward from a single point in heaven. The pillar below the pyramidion is the expression in stone of a common sight in the desert, a shaft of sunlight gleaming down to touch the earth through a rift in the clouds.

In Egypt the form evolved from cairn-like obeliskoid constructions of many dressed stones to the true monolithic obelisk. The 170-metre-high Washington Monument in Washington, DC, has the shape of an obelisk, but is constructed of limestone blocks. For the Ancient Egyptians the true power of the obelisk lay in the fact that it was a single, monolithic piece of stone, and they expanded their technology to allow the raising of larger and larger granite needles. The Egyptian obelisks that we know today range in size from miniature models found in tombs to the vast and ultimately unwieldy Unfinished Obelisk of Aswan, 41.75 metres long and weighing 1193 tonnes. The best-known Egyptian obelisks (which now stand in cities far from Egypt) range in size from 21 metres to 32 metres and weigh between 195 and 409 tonnes. We had in mind to raise a 9-metre obelisk weighing around 20 tonnes.

READING THE ROCK

Our schedule and our budget allowed us only three weeks of filming. To prepare for this critically short period, our team of engineering explorers travelled 600 miles up the Nile to the pink granite quarries of Aswan that yielded up the original obelisks. The team from the pyramid project were reunited: Egyptologist Mark Lehner, stonemason Roger Hopkins and ancient technology aficionado and sculptor Martin Isler. We were joined later by a tall, august Egyptian called Ali el Gasab, a foreman at the government's Luxor sites and a specialist in moving large antiquities. We had all visited the mummy of Ramses the Great in the Cairo Museum and had been struck by the resemblance between Ali's dark and expressive face and the old Pharaoh.

Our first task was to find a shaft of granite about 9 metres long to be our experimental obelisk. Until we had scrabbled over rock faces in half a dozen quarries we didn't know how hard it would be. Several times we thought we had it, but then Roger or one of the quarry workers would point out a lurking fault in the stone. We were about to resort to a reinforced concrete obelisk when our tireless 'fixer' Hossam Ali led us to a modern quarry a few hundred metres above the ancient quarry that still held the Unfinished Obelisk captive in its stone. Near the entrance was the reassuring sight of a giant, brand-new bulldozer and in the background was the rhythmic beat of granite-cutting gang saws. Then we saw a smooth, flawless wall of pink granite. We knew that our obelisk lay somewhere in that wall, if only we could free it from the bedrock in one piece.

We met the owner, Mr Hamada Rashwan, Aswan's 'king of granite'. Our first meeting set the pattern for the dozens that followed. It was interminable, and punctuated by many telephone calls, cups of tea and obscure references to engineering calculations involving sine and cosine. Late in the afternoon we came to the point, and Mr Hamada was confident that he could deliver our 9-metre obelisk. In fact, he could also supply a 13-metre obelisk. We could erect this at the entrance to his quarry as a memento of the project – and as a very prominent corporate symbol. We should have refused the offer, but it was just too tempting. We returned downriver with his promise that, when we returned in a couple of months, our two obelisks would be roughed out and waiting for us at the erection site by the main gates of the quarry. The 9-metre shaft would be our stand-by in case the big one broke.

A 13-metre obelisk is a formidable 40-tonne object, comparable to one of the smaller Ancient Egyptian obelisks. We had planned to explore the engineering concepts with a smaller model, so there was more than a little bravado in our confidence that we could raise the shaft within our three-week shooting schedule.

We returned to Egypt a month before filming had to commence. Our 9-metre block had been hewn from the granite bedrock, but work on the 13-metre needle had not even begun. We should have abandoned the big obelisk, but foolishly we had set our hearts on an epic task. We asked Mr Hamada to put all his efforts into preparing the large obelisk. In the meantime, Roger would try his hand at cutting out a 3-metre obelisk by ancient means.

Granite is hard and heavy – precisely why it is premium building material. In addition to hammers and steel chisels, Mr Hamada assailed the rock with high-temperature gas torches, diamond-bit drills, winches and steel cable, bulldozers and a 50-tonne Russian crane in order to rough out and manoeuvre our obelisk 50 metres up the hill. Even so his workers were stretched to their limits to deliver.

THE UNFINISHED OBELISK

Our first practical lesson in obelisks was a comparison of ancient and modern work: we contrasted Mr Hamada's mechanized frenzy, as his men struggled to complete the job, with the crude tools and heavy manual labour of ancient quarry workers. From our modern perspective, the sweat and time and man-hours invested by the Ancient Egyptians to bring a 40-metre monolith out of a granite ledge is baffling.

What did they work with? Great tracts of desert are strewn with the obelisk-makers' principal tools: dolerite balls. Artifacts of an ancient sea that once covered this region, these are water-rolled orbs of a mineral hard enough to chip granite. Given a red-ochre line to follow, a workman might swing a heavy 15–25-cm ball of dolerite, held in two hands or bound to some kind of shaft, and strike the rock surface to pound away a few grains of granite. With a thousand blows he could expect to create a little hollow and a handful of dust. Brushing this dust aside – the dust would cushion the blow and reduce the 'efficiency' of his tool – he could shift a ball's width to one side for the next thousand blows, and continue in this mind-numbing, muscle-tearing work in the stifling heat. Legislation on work-place conditions still lay three thousand years in the future and the ancient stoneworkers' only comfort was singing their equivalent of a sea shanty which was probably indistinguishable from the work chants we heard our twentieth-century quarry workers bawling as they hammered away at the stone. We know what the working environment would have been for the Pharaohs' workforce. The temperatures would have reached 120°F (49°C), and the air was surely white with fine granite dust. The few records we have suggest that 10 per cent of the workers died during the project.

Who were these men? Probably conscripted labourers, perhaps criminals and soldiers doing hard labour, together with skilled stone-cutters who created the hieroglyphs. We learn most about the ancient workers and their trials from one of their greatest failures: the Unfinished Obelisk of Aswan, which was close to our own site. This was not only the largest obelisk ever attempted, but would have been the largest single piece of stone ever moved in the history of engineering. After perhaps a year of cutting a trench around the gargantuan shaft a disastrous flaw was uncovered in the granite – a flaw that would have weakened the integrity of the obelisk and made it impossible to move or mount. We can see the outlines of smaller obelisk designs inscribed over the larger plan in an effort to make use of some of the enormous effort that had been expended; but in the end the year's work was declared a failure. We do not know which Pharaoh ordered this

OPPOSITE The Nile at Aswan. BELOW RIGHT The massive Unfinished Obelisk.
BELOW LEFT Mr Hamada Rashwan's men working with modern equipment.
BOTTOM LEFT Roger and his team using dolerite balls.

ambitious monument, nor the name of the hapless engineer who travelled despondently down the Nile to his god-king to bring the bad news. But we can appreciate the gift they inadvertently left us: a work in progress, abandoned in mid-stroke four millennia ago, with the marks of the tools and the measuring lines still in place.

The great shaft is still bound to the rock and lies at an angle in an uplift of granite. Its form is clear, the upper face is nearly smoothed and its pyramidion is roughly sculpted away from the granite. It is plain that grading away the shale in search of flawless stone had to be the obelisk-makers' first job.

WORKING THE QUARRY

Having drawn the outline of a 3-metre obelisk in a promising outcrop of granite in a distant corner of Mr Hamada's quarry, Roger and five of his Egyptian crew set to with the greenish black dolerite balls. They bashed at the hard granite for several days, sitting hunched over the rock face and swinging the 4.5-kg balls. Their visible progress, as it would have been for their ancient forebears, was insignificant. Nevertheless a small carpet of rough-dressed stone face had been cleared and levelled before the Egyptian workforce abandoned historical research for other pursuits and stopped turning up for work.

In an attempt to speed up progress Roger built a small, hot fire right on the granite. The heat expands the surface stone, which sloughs away from the cooler layers below in thin, plate-sized sheets the equivalent of two to three hours' pounding. Mark found quantities of charcoal at the site of the Unfinished Obelisk which could have been left over from ancient attempts at burning granite. By now Roger had had enough of dolerite balls and handed back the task of carving the 3-metre obelisk to Mr Hamada.

Sand that covered the site until recent times has preserved red ochre lines that allotted 60-cm lengths of trench to each worker or team of workers. Mark's observations confirmed those of Ronald Englebach, the British Egyptologist who studied this site most carefully in the 1920s. The labourers would have pounded to about 3.5 metres, and then the truly murderous work would have begun: they would have lain on their sides and swung the dolerite balls horizontally. Fewer men could have done this work, because men lying down take up more trench space, and less force could have been brought to bear on the balls. Cutting horizontally beneath the obelisk would have been slow torture in the still, baking atmosphere – half air, half dust – under the granite. This single underface would have occupied at least as much time as both vertical faces. The crews would have worked from both sides towards the middle, shoring up the obelisk's overhanging lower face with cribbing and wedges until they could feel the blows of the crews from the other side, tapping through a thinning spine of stone.

At this delicate point the old Egyptian workforce may have removed the shoring from one side and levered the other side until the obelisk – still whole, they would have prayed – split from the rock face. In this quarry, near the impossibly large Unfinished Obelisk, Roger and Mark found several spines that were probably the final earth-ties of successful obelisks.

While crews were still pounding out the side trenches, finish masons would have been kneeling at the top surface, smoothing and truing it. They would have used simple, sure tools. Try-squares would gauge the right-angle between faces. Taut strings dipped in red ochre slurry would have transferred a straight line on to the granite, much as masons and carpenters snap a dusty chalk line today. The flatness of a surface could be tested by pressing down a wide board coated with gummy ochre; they would beat away the red-touched stone and try the board again until the whole surface was red. Modern dentists fit fillings in a similar way, asking the patient to bite down on a strip of paper coated with blue powder, then burring away the areas of filling material that have been touched with blue. The 'truth' of the long face could be tested with T-gauges: the inverted cross-bars of several gauges would be placed along the surface in a line, and the engineer would sight across their vertical bars to discover whether any section of the face slanted left or right. First the top face, then – perhaps as the undercutting work continued beneath their feet – the other faces would be brought to a polish: trial and error, slow and careful, skill and judgement.

TOOLS AND TECHNIQUES

All the faces of the ancient obelisks are smooth and highly polished. Roger was attempting to smooth-dress only a patch of granite. He used the dolerite balls to define the surface and then ground it with a slurry of sand under a heavy stone scouring block. After hundreds of grating figures-of-eight, a splash of water revealed the beginnings of a polish.

Roger speculated whether the Ancient Egyptians started with dolerite, then moved to gradually softer stones such as sandstone and limestone – much as we might today move through increasingly finer grades of sandpaper – to achieve the final polish. The carving of the 2.5-cm-deep hieroglyphs, still crisp and clear three thousand years on, also posed questions. Even with modern tools and diamond wheels it would be difficult to emulate the quality of the ancient workmanship.

This is the subtle way in which an object as simple as an obelisk opens up tantalizing mysteries from the past. In this case the mystery involves metallurgy. The most useful metals of Ancient Egypt were copper alloys. Bronze, a relatively simple alloy of copper and tin, is an index of the technological sophistication of the time. It is a durable metal, but soft. A very few iron implements have been found in the tombs. Iron is much harder, but difficult to produce. It was probably used for ceremonial items, and regarded almost as a precious metal. It is fairly certain that the quarry workers of Aswan had no iron chisels. Yet Roger was beginning to notice rows of neat rectangular slots cut into granite outcrops all over Aswan: their size, depth and appearance indicating that only an iron chisel could have created them. To Roger's disappointment, however, Mark told us that an extensive new archaeological study suggests that they date from later times when Egypt was a Roman colony and hard metal chisels were widely available.

Even today, metallurgy is an art as much as a science. With the help of a small back-street foundry Roger spent several days trying to cast and then temper a bronze chisel that would cut granite. All his attempts failed – the granite blunted the chisels after a couple of hammer blows – but he did achieve success in casting a bronze drill and a saw that would cut the hard rock. Actually, it was quartz sand in a slurry of gypsum that did the cutting – the bronze tools only directed the cut.

A 5-cm tube twirled with a bow-shaped wooden handle moved the slurry to drill a hole, while a strip of bronze fitted with end-handles like a two-man saw worked the slurry in a linear way to make a cut. In the Cairo Museum, Mark found evidence of quartz sand and gypsum in a saw cut that was being used to remove the top of a granite sarcophagus.

Bronze drills like these could have been used to bore holes and hollows in sculptures and create some of the circular hieroglyph symbols. Mark experimented with another method that used only stone tools. During the research trip, prior to filming, Mark had noticed in the tomb of the Theban noble Rekhmire an unusual painting which shows two sculptors using what appear to be small pieces of stone to carve a granite statue. Small, dolerite hammers might make the kind of incised carving in the hieroglyphs. He marked out a doughnut-shaped form as a pattern, then bashed for hours within the lines. He then scraped around the impact-pocked edges with chips of hard quartzite and sandstone. Sinking this small hieroglyph 2.5 cm into granite would demand half a day's work, but we know how little time meant to the Pharaoh's artisans. Mark was convinced.

It seems likely that the obelisk, after being detached from the bedrock below, was rolled over 90° so that the lower, undressed face was accessible for smoothing. A half-finished sarcophagus and pharaonic statue in the quarries suggested that a lot of fine work was done on monuments while they were still there.

Before or after the rolling, a strong sled with smooth runners would have been lashed to the long, brittle stone. To begin the trip, the cradle runners were probably lowered on to a track made from a pair of smooth-topped timbers the same width apart. The timbers ran along the top of an earthwork causeway, blocked and ballasted as level as a railway track to make the journey from the quarry to the Nile as easy as possible.

OVERCOMING INERTIA

Our 3-metre, 2-tonne obelisk would be our test-run for the 13-metre obelisk that stubbornly remained in the quarry. We began to explore the problem of moving the long, heavy stone. Did the Ancient Egyptians use rollers or slippery fat under the sled? Roger favoured wooden rollers on a wooden trackway as the simplest and easiest solution but Martin Isler opposed the idea. He felt that rollers would make the sled difficult to control and would require a smooth surface in order to work properly.

Ali el Gasab's team of pullers had just arrived and Roger quickly seized the opportunity to train them. Martin needed the small stone to test some of his theories, and took a dim view of the way Ali and his men were handling the brittle granite.

In this initial confrontation Martin and Ali were natural antagonists: Martin short, fair and passionate when arguing about ancient engineering; Ali tall, dark and graceful, a natural performer and leader. Ali and Martin did not share a spoken or philosophical language. They made faces at each other and waved their hands threateningly, they pointed and shouted, they demanded that Mark should interpret their cautions and complaints to each other.

But Roger and Mark stood to one side. They had been through the first steps of training a pulling crew on the pyramid project and were confident that Ali, an impressive figure, could motivate his men.

THE GRAND BARGES

The quarries at Aswan were chosen not only for the quality of their stone but also for their proximity to the Nile: only water transport could carry such massive loads such long distances. The largest obelisks probably weighed around the 500-tonne mark, but New Kingdom Pharaohs also erected colossal monolithic statues of themselves weighing up to 1000 tonnes, which seemed to be the upper limit that the Ancient Egyptians could transport.

Modern wooden cargo boats have a stiff, heavy timber spine called a keel, into which are fitted heavy timber ribs that curve out and upwards to the deck level. Another large timber, the keelson, clamps down over the ribs to make a fairly rigid structure. The ribs are sheathed with thinner lengthwise planks which are caulked – the horizontal spaces between them are stuffed with cotton and oakum twine which expands with moisture and seals the hull. Such a boat uses the ribs to distribute the loads within it and can carry great weights. Egypt has never had great forests of the kind of large trees that provide timber for cargo ships like this. The wood from native Egyptian acacias and sycamores gives small planks, and so the earliest Egyptian boats had fairly flexible hulls made up of short, cleverly interlocking planks on very light connecting frames. A deck braced with stout thwarts was hung over this thin hull. The wide boat was stiffened longitudinally with ropes run lengthwise along Y-shaped struts above the deck and tightened by twisting – an arrangement that would later be called a hogging frame. These pieced-together hulls are delicate and break under uneven stresses. They must be loaded very carefully, and nothing can be carried below deck against the hull – everything is carried on the stiffened deck.

Cheryl Haldane, the nautical archaeologist in our team, believes that the Egyptians built great barges, to the specific measurements of each obelisk, within an earthen dry dock at the edge of the Nile. Her research suggests that an obelisk would need a round-bottomed, shallow-draught craft about 25 per cent longer than the needle itself, whose width was about a third of its length. The hull would have been supported by wooden buttresss and then the mud would have been packed to the level of the deck. She believes the causeway from the quarry was built out on to the deck of the barge; the obelisk was dragged from the quarry and on to the barge's deck. The hogging truss was set up above the obelisk once it was in place. The earth support was dug away from the loaded barge, in her scenario, and replaced by wooden buttresses. At the time of the Nile's annual flood, work-men broke the levee surrounding the dry dock to let water fill the basin and lift the great barge off its wooden supports. The craft, says Cheryl, was poled into the Nile and hauled downriver by a dozen or so rowing boats.

Roger remained unconvinced, arguing that the vessel would have been bogged down in mud rather than able to float off on the rising water. Cheryl and Roger also had opposing ideas about how the barge was loaded.

To demonstrate his scenario Roger gathered stones and sticks to construct two stone piers a barge-width apart, then dredged out a channel between them.

Roger demonstrates his barge transportation theory,
watched by Mark and Cheryl Haldane.

He dragged the little obelisk on its sled out on to one of the piers. For the dozens of 17-metre cedar beams imported from Lebanon that would have spanned the gap between the piers he laid two sticks across his loading channel. The obelisk's sled would have been side-levered on to the spanning timbers and slid or rolled out over the water. Roger believes the barge could have been ballasted with stones or sand to lie low enough in the water to creep under the obelisk. When the ballast was removed the barge might have risen to take the weight of the obelisk. Unfortunately for Roger, his model barge sprung a leak and instead of rising, it sank ignominiously.

There were, however, flaws in both plans. In Cheryl's scenario, stabilizing the hull by packing mud or shoring with wooden buttresses could never be an entirely satisfactory process. As the ponderous weight came down on the barge's deck the pieced-together hull, supported unevenly, would buckle, and planks would shear away from one another. Even a potato-sized rock in the mud would be driven through the hull by the enormous pressure – and even if the hull were undamaged, it would still be sitting on the bottom. If the Nile's level rose and fell the unevenly supported hull would surely be destroyed.

The flaw in Roger's model was that only the even pressure of the water could support the loaded hull safely. Loading the barge with ballast below the deck where the hull was not designed to carry such loads would have placed uneven weight on the delicately joined planks. The amount of ballast necessary to compensate for the weight of the obelisk would almost equal the weight of the obelisk. It is doubtful that the barge would even survive, much less hold out the water.

But we learned much from experimenting with these two theories. A third scenario was subsequently discussed that used Roger's piers and permanent stone dock. The barge was probably filled almost completely by baling in water. The half-sunk barge was towed between the piers with only a centimetre or two to spare between deck and spanning timbers. The barge's deck was carefully lined into optimum position to take the tremendous weight of the obelisk evenly and not cause any listing. At this point the water in the barge was baled out. The barge rose steadily and powerfully, with the hydraulic force of buoyancy in its favour, until it began to take the weight of the great stone. The bow-to-stern hogging trusses could remain in position throughout this procedure since the obelisk was loaded from the side of the boat. The trusses would have been tightened gradually as the hull took the immense strain. When the obelisk, hull and cross timbers floated free, carrying the whole weight, the stone could be levered and blocked up an inch or two, just enough to pull out the spanning timbers. The load could be lowered and lashed securely to the deck and hull, using the cradle and stone needle itself to provide additional stability to the structure of the barge.

THE HONOUR OF KINGS AND GODS

Where did the obelisks go? An area that is now a suburb of Cairo was one destina-tion. While Egypt was governed from many administrative capitals, Heliopolis was the spiritual centre of the country for much of its history. It was a place of priests and seers rather than rulers, and sacred to the sun god Ra. One of the few women who ruled Egypt, Queen Hatshepsut, reigned from Thebes. Her twenty-two-year reign was a period of peace and great artistic flowering. Hatshepsut's mortuary temple at Deir el-Bahri is one of Egypt's finest monuments. When her husband Tuthmosis II died in 1479 BC, before she produced a male heir, Hatshepsut be-came regent for her twelve-year-old stepson, Tuthmosis III. She obviously en-joyed the role because instead of stepping down when her stepson became old enough to rule she declared herself Pharaoh. She presented herself as both queen and king, appearing in statues and paintings not only as a woman but as a man with ceremonial chin-beard. She reigned with her stepson, Tuthmosis III, who used the horses and chariots brought to Egypt from Asia by the Hyskos as effective weapons in his widespread imperial conquests. The wealth of tribute brought back from his victories abroad paid for marvellous temples at Luxor and Heliopolis. One each of a pair of his obelisks now stand in New York and London.

Tuthmosis III was a great warrior but may have been more loyal to his con-cubine mother, Isis, than to his royal stepmother. Sometime after Hatshepsut's death he systematically chiselled her name out of every public monument in a near-complete attempt to erase her name from history. Tuthmosis even went to the ridiculous length of building a sandstone wall around her Karnak obelisks, leaving just the gold-plated pyramidions exposed.

The mightiest builder of the ancient world was the 19th Dynasty Pharaoh Ramses II, better known as Ramses the Great, an almost fanatical creator of temples and monuments – mostly to himself. One of his colossi – once over 17 metres high and weighing about 1000 tonnes – lies ruined in the courtyard of the Ramesseum, his mortuary temple in Thebes. It bears his religious name, User-maat-Re, translated by the Greek historian Diodorus as 'Ozymandias'. The imperial coolness of the face, the formal pose and the ruined remnants of this once-mighty Pharaoh inspired the British Romantic poet, Shelley. His poem 'Ozymandias' ends:

> *'My name is Ozymandias, king of kings:*
> *Look on my works, ye Mighty, and despair!'*
> *Nothing beside remains. Round the decay*
> *Of that colossal wreck, boundless and bare*
> *The lone and level sands stretch far away.*

Ramses II commissioned several obelisks, but he appropriated many more from previous Pharaohs by simply having royal stonemasons carve his cartouche, his 'signature', in the granite. When he had a pair of obelisks made for himself, in anticipation of similar guile on the part of rulers to come, he had his name chiselled into the butt of the obelisks where they rested against their pedestals. No one could see this carving of his name, nor, even if they did, could they remove it. This crafty vanity came to light when, many centuries later, the French moved one of his obelisks to Paris.

Ramses II expanded the temples at Luxor to a magnificent extent, but his most soaring work is the cliff temple on the Nile at Abu Simbel in Nubia, at the southern gateway to Ancient Egypt. An entire sandstone cliff facing the Nile is sculpted as a temple facade with giant images of himself and his favourite wife Nefartari, 'for whose sake the very sun does shine'. This was the temple saved from the rising waters behind the High Dam at Aswan in the 1960s. International efforts headed by the United States lifted the cliff face in sections over 30 metres to safety, with engineering feats that match the building of the pyramids.

From our present-day perspective the self-adoring monuments of Pharaohs may seem vain and ridiculous, but they and their subjects thought about them in a very different way. The pyramids, elaborate votive temples, jewelled sarcophagi, hidden tombs and intricately created mummies were directed toward the preservation of a mystic duality called the ka, a bond between the physical person of the Pharaoh and a royal, immortal spirit. As long as the person of the Pharaoh – his name, the record of his deeds, his lineage and his body – was still prominent as a vessel for the spirit, the ka could bring good fortune to the land and its people.

Queen Hatshepsut's obelisk at Karnak.
INSET The head of the Queen who was often represented as
a king complete with ceremonial beard.

The monument graveyard at Tanis.

Ramses was serving a sacred trust, then, in setting up his face and statue on the land. If his reign was fortunate (and, in a place where a long growing season graces a long, fertile valley, things often seemed fortunate) he had a duty to preserve the ka and its power for his people. It was in their best interests to help him.

Ramses II built his capital in the pleasant delta of the Nile, along one of the eastern channels. We know that it was an engineered delight with ponds and terraces and monuments of every kind. We know that it contained many temples and many obelisks. But his ka failed him. The Nile changed its course, history meandered away from Ramses' dynasty, and when Alexander the Great took Egypt in 332 BC the magnificent city of Pi-Ramses was lost. Its many monuments were looted for building stone and used in the new capital of Tanis, the graveyard of obelisks, where twenty-two of Ramses' obelisks lie prostrate today at the end of their millennia-long journey down the Nile from Aswan. The old trip was about 560 miles downstream to Heliopolis, but many obelisks have made longer and more eventful journeys.

ROMAN PRIZES

It has been suggested that in ancient times well over fifty obelisks exceeded 10 metres in length. We shall never know how many walls in Cairo are buttressed with sacred monoliths, since in the Middle Ages the glories of Heliopolis were regarded essentially as a convenient stone quarry. The pyramids were in perfect condition (barring a tomb robber's hole here and there) until about AD 1200, when enterprising builders began to harvest their polished limestone casing for Cairo's construction. Some half a dozen obelisks still stand upright in Egypt today, half of which were re-erected in recent times in Cairo. Another thirteen were carried away centuries ago to imperial Rome; they include the largest surviving obelisk, the 32-metre, 451-tonne Lateran, which stands in Piazza San Giovanni. The Romans took another to the early Christian city of Constantinople. One is in the Place de la Concorde in Paris, one on the Embankment in London, and the last obelisk to leave Egypt resides in Central Park in New York City.

The practical Romans used their obelisks as markers along the spina – the dividing spine of a chariot racecourse – and even as gnomons for giant sundials, surmounting the pyramidions with head-sized golden balls that cast the hour-shadow. The ball at the top of the obelisk that marked the *spina* of Nero's Circus Gianus supposedly contained the ashes of Julius Caesar: a nice tale, but the ball was empty when it was opened during the Renaissance. Fetched from Egypt at the orders of the Emperors Caligula and Claudius around AD 50, this was the only obelisk that had remained upright since the days of the Empire. In 1585 the energetic Pope Sixtus V decided to use it as an icon of Christianity's victory over paganism. Moving it to a prominent site in front of St Peter's cathedral had been discussed for many years by many engineers. The obelisk was 25.3 metres high and its weight was calculated at a little over 339 tonnes. The task of moving it a mere 250 metres – after its progress of thousands of miles over two millennia – was enormous: the difficulties of its first move had been overcome by the accumulated experience of Egyptian engineers; the second move was accomplished with dispatch by regiments of Roman sappers: the third was approached timorously by Renaissance architects.

Their difficulties were the same as ours. The great hurdle is not the obelisk's weight. Weight can always be managed, somehow; we moved the 40-tonne horizontal obelisk without incident. The combination of the obelisk's slender proportions, the brittleness of its material and its ponderous weight make it vulnerable when shifted suddenly. If a beam fails or a rope breaks, the load will be concentrated unevenly and the slim stem will snap. When quarrying, transporting and raising an obelisk any force must be applied evenly to avoid creating dynamic stresses that would shatter the stone.

From a field of largely fanciful schemes, the Pope selected a sound plan by the brilliant Swiss engineer Domenico Fontana. Using modular cross-braced towers as high purchase points, he lowered the shaft from its old position using miles of hemp rope and multiple-block pulleys made fast to iron bands bolted together at many points along the obelisk's length. The ropes fanned out to forty timber capstans where eight hundred men and seventy-five horses turned them to signals given by cannon-shot, drum and bell. The now horizontal shaft was moved by sled along a timber causeway to the new site, where the modular towers were re-erected and new capstans were set up. Pope Sixtus was so worried by the whole business that he decreed absolute silence during the re-erection of the obelisk, on threat of death, as well as ordering two special masses and personally blessing Fontana. Once again hundreds of men turned the capstans in response to signals. The obelisk rose on to new bronze astragals – four raised brackets, one on each corner, that permitted supports under the butt end to remain in position until erection was complete. These astragals are shaped like crabs in honour of the Roman sun god Apollo, a reference in turn to the Egyptian sun god Ra. This time, however, the obelisk's pyramidion was topped not by a golden ball but by a cross.

Fontana's success turned Pope Sixtus V into a compulsive obelisk resurrector. Within three years Fontana's method raised three more forgotten obelisks for him. Sixtus had started another obelisk craze: no Baroque papacy was complete without one.

Fontana is one of the bright lights in the obelisk saga; he may even be the first modern engineer. His plans for dealing with the ancient stone were comprehensive and his record of the project was full of detail, down to explanatory

Swiss engineer Domenico Fontana's plan of how he
proposed to raise the Roman obelisk for Pope Sixtus V.

engravings, the costs of labour and equipment, tables for scheduling and communication, plans of tools and tower cross-bracing, research into material strengths and properties (such as shrinkage, compression, and deformation), considerations for reusing the modular equipment, and critical notes on the failures he encountered. Why did none exist before? One reason was that the ancient engineers possessed a professional confidence and modesty foreign to us. Their Pharaoh ordered them to accomplish a feat and they did so. They did not regard success as unusual, nor did they conceive that anyone would be just as interested in the process as in the result.

A watercolour of the Luxor temple entrance, painted in 1800
by François Charles Cecile, showing both of Ramses II's obelisks in
position. The one on the right was sent to Paris in 1831.

'BRING ME BACK A LITTLE OBELISK'

The modern fascination with Egypt probably began during Napoleon's failed campaign there in 1798–1801, when troops returning to France brought with them sketches and accounts of wonders in the romantic desert. Josephine had asked Napoleon to 'bring her back a little obelisk' and he wanted to oblige. The most important object he brought back, though, was secured by an artillery officer named Bouchard: a black stone about the size of an armchair cushion bearing three inscriptions – one in hieroglyphics, one in demotic script and one in Greek. We know it today as the Rosetta Stone after the place where it was found, and the parallel inscriptions enabled the cryptographer and linguist Jean François Champollion to unlock the door of hieroglyphics and let us peer into the ancient world. In 1830, with the approval of the Egyptian ruler, the khedive, Champollion himself picked an obelisk for France. It was an unfortunate choice because it was one of the only pair of obelisks still standing in front of a temple with matching pairs of sphinxes and statues, as originally installed at the temple in Luxor by the monument's owner, Ramses the Great. An outbreak of cholera hampered the work of French marine engineers, who encased the shaft in a 13-cm thickness of soft pine and lowered it using multiple shear legs and naval tackle designed by Apollinaire le Bas. Its 23-metre length was dragged into the specially built barge *Luxor*, designed to take it along the coastal waters of France and up the Seine to Paris. Two hundred and forty men manning five capstans dragged it out of the *Luxor* and up a ramp on to the intended site; in 1836 le Bas set new shear legs and raised the shaft on to a new pedestal of Breton stone.

THE SHIPWRECKED STONE

Britain was awarded its own obelisk after combined British and Turkish forces recaptured Alexandria from Napoleon in 1801. One of a pair that had been brought from Heliopolis and set up by the Romans at the water entrance to the Caesareum, the temple to the deified Julius Caesar, in Alexandria. It had fallen into the sand during an earthquake in the early fourteenth century.

The first attempt to take it home failed when a captured French frigate that was intended to haul it was destroyed by a storm, and it was not until 1867 that an engineer named John Dixon brought it to London. He constructed a modular, watertight cast-iron cylinder 29 metres long and 4.6 metres in diameter, which was bolted and braced around the obelisk. Timber wheels were then bolted and banded around the cylinder and the iron tube was rolled into the sea, where it floated away from the land. The timber wheels were dismantled, a bridge, ballast, keels and steadying sails added, and the cylinder was towed out into the Mediterranean as the barge *Cleopatra*.

In the Bay of Biscay a storm shifted the Cleopatra's ballast and the barge turned on to her beam end. A rescue boat from the tug *Olga* was sent, but foundered in the storm with the loss of six lives. *Olga* herself then steamed dangerously close to the *Cleopatra* and brought off her crew, but abandoned the 'sinking' cast-iron contraption. After the storm, the *Cleopatra* was found in good

The beginning of a journey – London's obelisk is launched
at Alexandria inside John Dixon's cast-iron cylinder.

condition by another steamer; after her ballast had been redistributed, she was towed to England and, after a demand for exorbitant salvage payments, brought up the Thames to London. Dixon clasped the obelisk around its middle with a cast-iron belt, stirruped to its base and fitted with pivot blades at its centre of gravity. He raised and shifted it to a point above its intended new site on the Embankment and lowered the pivot blades on to iron fulcrums. When the horizontal timber supports were removed the shaft was swung to the vertical and lowered on to its base – three new crab astragals of bronze joined one original Roman crab. Monolith and crabs sat on a pedestal engraved with the customary illustrious names, including those of the engineer Dixon – ruined by the cost of his inventive, involved and star-crossed plans – and the six lost sailors. With enthusiastic disregard for historical accuracy the new addition to London's skyline was christened Cleopatra's Needle.

THE YANKEE NEEDLE

The last obelisk to leave Egypt was the partner to the one that had been brought to London. This pair of obelisks had originally been set at the temple of Atum in Heliopolis by Tuthmosis III in 1461 BC, though both carried additional self-congratulation by Ramses II and a small inscription by the late Pharaoh Orsoken I (22nd Dynasty, 933 BC). The western face of the obelisk that was about to be transported thousands of miles away had been roughened by the effects of a fire started by the Persian invader Cambyses when he sacked Heliopolis in 525 BC. In 1878, the politically impotent and commercially agreeable ruler of Egypt gave this obelisk to the USA.

A young naval officer, Lieutenant Commander Henry H. Gorringe, was sent to bring it back, but the controlling foreign element in Alexandria put every conceivable obstacle in his way. But land disputes, claims for reparations that cited the obelisk as collateral, and refusal of moving permits did not deter him. One of his first acts was to barricade the site, set a guard and place the American flag on the pyramidion, giving notice that the monument was United States property.

Gorringe set up a prefabricated cast-iron frame around the shaft. An iron harness of steel bands was tightened around the girth in several places and a two-cable suspension truss was tightened on one side. The harness was linked to a belt of iron with trunnions at the balance point and lifted with the great stone on to mating pivots in the frame. By means of this elegant device the obelisk was to pivot smoothly horizontally, its suspension truss lifting 30 tonnes of bending shear from both ends and distributing the massive load along its length. But, as the obelisk began to rotate, the two men controlling the movement were unnerved by loud creaking sounds. This led one of them to stop abruptly, causing the tackle to break. In a moment the obelisk swung down out of control, bouncing twice on the stack of timbers before coming to rest in a horizontal position. The cribbing that saved the obelisk was then removed in stages as the stone was lowered by hydraulic jacks.

Foreign interests blocked Gorringe's sensible plan to take a one-mile passage across the town's isthmus to the steamer *Dessoug*'s berth. He was forced to drag the

The end of a journey – New York's obelisk is raised into position
using Gorringe's frame and trunnion device.

obelisk through dangerous surf, on to a pontoon barge, and tow it 10 miles round to the steamer's dry dock. There he removed the steamer's bow and slid the shaft into the bilges, where it was cushioned with pine and blocked into place with oak timbers. Its original pedestal was lowered into the *Dessoug's* cargo hold, using the two largest cranes in Alexandria. The *Dessoug's* bow was replaced and the obelisk reached New York a few weeks later.

At Staten Island the obelisk was slid out, placed on a barge and towed across the Hudson River to the West 96th Street dock of Manhattan. Winched off the barge and up the river bank, it was strapped into place on a timber cradle with its own steam donkey engine. Obelisk and engine were rolled along H-section beams on cannonball bearings until the great weight of the stone began to split the beams. After that it moved on simple rollers, its donkey engine winding up cable that ran through steel pulleys made fast to cable anchors in the street ahead.

The obelisk, now called, like its London counterpart, 'Cleopatra's Needle', made its way through the city streets for 112 days until it reached its site in Central Park behind the Metropolitan Museum of Art, where Gorringe's original frame and trunnion device, reassembled on site, allowed the massive shaft to pivot away from its horizontal timber causeway and be lowered on to its pedestal of Aswan granite. On 15 January 1881 it was situated to face the sun at the precise angle that the priests of Amun-Ra had decreed thousands of years before.

LESSONS

From the travels of these old stones we learned that human muscle, intelligently applied, can raise obelisks. Later mechanical developments and materials that had been unavailable to the Ancient Egyptians eased the task enormously. Fontana enjoyed the advantages of the block-and-tackle and the capstan, two machines unknown to the Egyptians. Dixon and Gorringe were able to use the durability and strength of cast iron to carry a load, and hydraulic power to raise and lower it.

But our task was to explore Egyptian engineering. We were restricted to wood, stone, cordage, levers, wedges and inclined planes. We learned that even simple mechanical advantage can multiply motive power to lift and move the most enormous weights.

We learned that friction was the first and easiest obstacle to overcome. We concluded that greased skids were the most likely method to succeed, but that rollers had also been used in Ancient Egypt.

We learned that every obelisk mover took enormous pains to support the length of the shaft evenly and to control its positioning on the pedestal. The Cecil B. De Mille method of tipping the unsupported obelisk into place in one rolling swoop over the curved edge of a ramp is cinematically impressive but structurally disastrous. It is unlikely that the Ancient Egyptian builders constructed trusses or casing around their obelisks to take a portion of the stresses during activities such as rotating an obelisk on its centre of gravity or lifting it at one end. Whatever their method, they must not have exceeded the strength limitations of Aswan granite.

Such knowledge only comes from long experience, which was the Ancient Egyptians' greatest mechanical advantage. We were searching too quickly for experience. Three weeks is not long enough to re-create an entire engineering discipline, not even with a lot of library time and armchair conjecture.

A MODEL EFFORT

Our first attempt at raising an obelisk, was made with the 2-tonne one. Impulsive and quick to judge, Martin Isler was also observant and inventive and had great respect for the original craftsmen. He believed in simplicity – small gains repeated over and over. He wanted to try hauling without rollers and the workmen obliged him, partly because he had asked them to eat dozens of bananas, a favourite fruit of theirs. The small obelisk's sled was lowered on to the timber rails with the banana skins in front. The runners pushed most of the peels out of the way. But it seemed to work; the lubricant was as slippery under this 2-tonne monolith as it was under the shoes of the cops chasing Charlie Chaplin. The obelisk slid along the ramp until the butt reached its pedestal.

Martin had identified one of the most important mechanical features present in every monument we had found: the turning groove. Every obelisk base we had examined had a notch that received one of the obelisk's butt edges when it was slid on to the pedestal at an angle. The groove held the edge and acted as a hinge for turning the obelisk upright, positioning the obelisk at its exact angle to the rising sun and preventing the stone from sliding across the pedestal. Positioning the obelisk precisely into its turning groove from a ramp is a prime requisite of a successful raising. Twisting the upright obelisk on its base to reorient it would be virtually impossible. Hatshepsut's obelisk at Karnak is witness to this problem: it sits slightly twisted and beyond the turning groove. After the Egyptians, all obelisk erectors from the Romans onward placed the butt of the shaft on astragals.

Martin's plan was based in part on a method used in Seringapatam in India in 1805, when six hundred men levered up a slim 34-tonne 17-metre obelisk in memory of a Dr Webb. As at Seringapatam, Martin's first priority was to place the

Raising the 2-tonne obelisk: pulling it along the track
towards the turning groove, and using levers and ropes to pull
it upright once it was in the groove.

butt edge of the horizontal obelisk carefully into the pedestal turning groove. He
placed teams of workers in a semi-circle around the upper end of the obelisk, and
they started to lever it up towards the vertical. Each angular gain of a centimetre or
two was locked in with wedges and blocking behind the stone, and a haphazard
embankment of earth, stone and wood started to grow beneath the rising obelisk.
When the angle had reached 40°, lines were attached just below the pyramidion.
Some lines led forward to pull the obelisk upright; others led back to stop it being
pulled over its centre of gravity; and a pair of lines stretched to the sides to control
it further. After a few hearty 'heave-hos' the obelisk tipped up handsomely,
accompanied by much applause.

'Thank you, thank you all,' said Martin, warmed by the appreciation. But we
all knew that this was our smallest obelisk.

Roger's sandpit method. Guiding the obelisk's
butt into the turning groove was the main problem.

DANGERS OF THE PIT

Roger proposed another method to raise the 40-tonne obelisk. He planned to tip
it upright by letting the butt sink down from a high causeway into a sandpit. This
scheme had been suggested by the energetic British Egyptologist Englebach in
the 1920s. He proposed that the obelisks had been drawn up a ramp and along a
causeway to a point above their pedestals. The causeway – indeed much of the
necessary earthwork for moving great weights in Ancient Egypt – would have
been built of bricks made of dried mud, the most common building material in
Egypt even today. The causeway would have ended in a stout mudbrick box filled
about three-quarters full of sand. The obelisk and its supporting sled would have
been tipped gradually over the curve of the down-ramp at its balance point until

it rested on the sand. At the bottom of the sandpit, openings would have been unplugged, allowing the fine sand to flow out like water. The level of sand in the pit would have dropped, and the obelisk would have sunk slowly down. The sled would have rotated on the near edge of the brick sandpit, tipping more vertically as the sand drained and the falling level took the butt of the obelisk down with it. Using the 'hydraulic' pressure of the sand to control the obelisk's descent would have been a clever use of the stone's own weight. Once engaged in the turning groove the obelisk would have been not too far from upright, perhaps at an angle of 55°. From this angle, lines could have persuaded the tall shaft to rise to an upright position.

Mr Hamada, the quarry owner, had objections to our trying out Englebach's idea. Roger, he pointed out, had only one objective: to get the obelisk upright come what may. But as the owner of the quarry he felt his prime concern must be for the safety of his employees. Roger assured Mr Hamada that he too would be risking life and limb down in the pit, but Mr Hamada remained worried. As a result, we amended our already curtailed plans. Roger would first build a small sandpit and make a practice run with the 2-tonne obelisk. A deep box was laid up around the grooved pedestal with big mud bricks. Sand ports at the bottom were stopped off by smaller bricks. The pit was filled with sand and the obelisk moved forward until the centre of gravity was reached and the sled tipped into the sand.

Martin did not see how they could possibly find the turning groove by pushing sand away from one side to the other. But Roger disagreed and got the men going: they pulled the bricks away from the ports and sand streamed out which they continually shovelled away to make room for more. The obelisk sank and tipped up, just as he had hoped. But then the butt veered off to one side and it stopped. Roger's discouragement at this point was not helped by Martin reiterating his contempt of the idea. Roger tried – in vain – to free it with a long-handled shovel. Then, despite Mr Hamada's cautions, one of the workmen decided he would crawl into a sandport until only his legs were visible. We watched nervously. A sudden puff of dust was followed by the man reversing crab-like, at astonishing speed, and then a gush of sand. Roger was delighted to inform us, especially Martin, that the obelisk was now practically over the turning groove!

While this method might have worked for the Ancient Egyptians, how could the great obelisks have been guided unerringly to their intended position under the sand? Did a chute carry the sled down to the pedestal's turning groove? We knew the original builders had used sand to lower heavy weights, but what we didn't have was centuries of experience. Clearly they didn't go down blindly towards the turning groove.

FALLBACK

Soon the quarry became alive with activity. The men were not working with us, however, but were busy sweeping up, painting outbuildings and stencilling Hamada's company name on everything in sight, including on a massive billboard right next to where the obelisk would stand, perfectly placed for every camera angle. We wanted to make use of every hour of daylight in an attempt to achieve our goal, but great preparations were clearly being made for some other event.

We now discovered that Mr Hamada had become an experimental archaeologist as well as a quarry manager. He had decided that we were wrong and had announced to the district governor that he was ready to solve the mystery of how his quarrymen ancestors raised these impossible objects.

The governor arrived in an air-conditioned Mercedes and stepped into the bright sun wearing a pin-striped suit, followed by aides, press and cameramen. This was a photo opportunity. After much smiling and shaking of hands, Mr Hamada proudly led the governor to a model of his obelisk erection scheme. Like us, he proposed to use a sandpit – but not for the obelisk. In his scheme the obelisk had already been slid down on to the pedestal and turning groove, and was attached by ropes to a huge rock weight sitting on a sandpit in front of it. The sand flowed out, the rock descended, and its weight, passing over a sturdy A-frame, pulled the obelisk upright. In model form this was a most impressive no-hands demonstration, as the obelisk rose all by itself once a trapdoor was opened under the sandpit holding the counterweight. More photo opportunities. But the governor had a busy schedule and, after further handshakes all around, it was back into the Mercedes, and the event was over. Mr Hamada was happy. He had glossed over the fact that the counterweight weighed as much as the obelisk and might not provide the fine control that human pullers could exert during the delicate phase of bringing an obelisk upright. We, however, had merely lost more time. Roger brooded and sketched new plans. Martin brooded and fulminated. Mark reread Englebach.

Ali walked up on to the ramp of the partially built sandpit. The 13-metre obelisk was sitting on sled and rollers behind him. He stood at the edge of the pit, a thin, serious man in a flapping, flowing *galabiyya,* lighting a cigarette in cupped hands and looking out over the desert. The breeze blew away the pungent Egyptian tobacco smoke. He was putting together an idea.

Time was short, and Ali's plan was clear and workable. It used one wall of the sandpit, with minor alterations. It used much of what we had learned. It was our best chance of success in the time we had left. After general consultation we decided to make our attempt using Ali's plan, and we tried to forget the fact that this might be the last time for many years that anyone would explore this fascinating problem in ancient engineering.

Roger's spirits were blunted when the sandpit plan was abandoned. He still believed it would work on the larger scale, but was too practical to waste time mourning the idea. He had a responsibility to fulfil: it was his job to prepare the obelisk's base, to make sure it sat solidly and absolutely level. Gravity was the only force that supported the obelisk – no steel bolts, no reinforcing rod, no props, just a true surface well founded. A well-set obelisk like those in London, Paris or New York could withstand up to 75 tonnes of wind pressure, four times as much as a hurricane could exert.

In the morning Ali's crew assembled. They worked with spirit, encouraged by Ali's shouting, singing, chaffing style. The men grasped the pulling lines and tried to start the obelisk rolling along the high causeway.

But the sled would not budge. Although its sturdy design was based on that of an ancient one in the Cairo Museum, we were worried that it was not evenly supported on the embankment and might buckle under the weight of our 40-tonne obelisk. We soon discovered, however, that it was the rollers rather than the sled that were causing the problem. The load had been sitting too long, and its

Ali's plan in action – 200 men pulling the 40-tonne
obelisk towards the incline, and Ali anxiously waving as it
teeters at its centre of gravity.

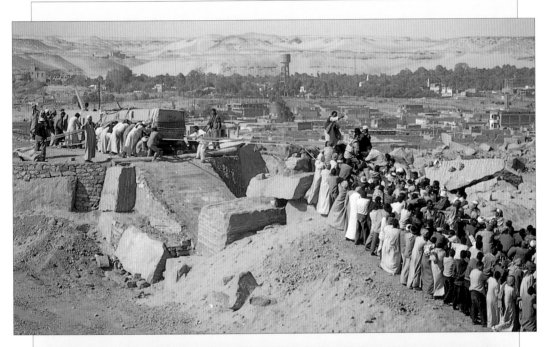

dead weight had compressed the rollers. Slightly flattened, they were reluctant to turn. Ali exhorted his team and they all pulled in unison, but to no avail. The rollers were shifted with blows from sledgehammers.

The huge weight moved, and rolled and the men laughed and sang, pulling faster and together. They were eager, too eager, and they pulled the sled and rollers to one side, off the timber track! Ali flew into a rage, his *galabiyya* whipping about him as his bony, expressive hands carved the air like scimitars about the neck of miscreants.

Levers were brought, and the crews pulled with all their strength. The sled was shouldered back on track. The obelisk approached the lip of the pit and its butt crept beyond the edge.

The causeway ended in a shallow downramp at an angle of about 32°: its purpose was to bring down the butt edge of the obelisk on its sled to meet the turning groove. Ali, Martin and Roger favoured a steeper descent of 45°, but Mr Hamada didn't believe we could hold back the weight of the obelisk at that angle. Behind the moving obelisk our thickest, 7-cm hawsers were laid back and turned about thick, round, horizontal timbers wedged behind pairs of large boulders located at the beginning of the causeway. Our hawsers were made of manilla hemp and were probably not too dissimilar in strength to ancient hawsers which were made of halfa grass or possibly date palm fibre. The friction of the hawsers against these snubbing timbers would check the obelisk's descent and control it. The butt now extended several feet beyond the edge, perilously close to the centre of gravity of the huge stone. Once it was at that point, equally balanced, things would happen swiftly.

The obelisk seemed to hesitate, the butt dipped, the pyramidion swung up. The movement was in reality slow but, to all of us clenching our teeth and breathing shallowly, seemed too fast. The great stone descended with a ponderous gesture and settled gently, with a grating of sand and pebbles. The check hawsers were holding.

There was both terrific excitement and terrific tension. Ali was shouting to the foreman of the check hawser team – a reliable older man, but quite deaf. Ali shouted again and his *galabiyya* flapped in agitation as he waved both arms. The team offered a little slack and the sled gave a few centimetres with a groan. More slack was followed by further groaning progress down the ramp.

Which is heavier, a weight going uphill or one going downhill? Moving downhill, a weight gains momentum and is heavier in proportion to its mass. We had 40 tonnes of mass generating unexpected momentum. The hawsers creaked, the sled tried to shift. Worst of all, the snubbing timbers around which the thick brake ropes were wrapped were being pulled up and out of their rock seats. If they rose another 25 cm they would lose their holding power and be snapped towards the obelisk like 500-kg projectiles, cutting down anything in their path, and the huge stone would career down the slide into the pedestal with a crash that would smash the obelisk. Men piled on to the end of the snubbing timbers to hold them in. The crews gave more slack. Roger had wanted to pack some clay above the pedestal to absorb energy should the brake ropes fail to hold the obelisk, which was suddenly on the move again – but this precaution had been forgotten. The crew tried a gentle snubbing action and increased the strain. Mercifully, it held just before the butt met the pedestal. Ali signalled again, and the obelisk was cut free from the sled. A nudge with a lever moved the butt down a few centimetres, then another and another. There was a grinding sound, and the obelisk had found its mark in the turning groove.

Ali nodded solemnly and his men danced around in jubilation. We were all delighted and we wanted to celebrate. But we had not raised an obelisk – not yet.

FRUSTRATION

After a break, the second part of Ali's plan was implemented. Using levers in rhythmic surges, the men tipped up the obelisk, centimetre by centimetre. Every upward gain they made was consolidated with wedges driven home between the obelisk and the sled. They shouted and sang. The great stone was rising.

But there came a point when it would not rise further. When the sled was tipped to about 40° levering became more and more inefficient. The ends of the levers were too high for the men to reach, and they had to try to bring them down

Trying to lever and pull the huge 40-tonne obelisk
into an upright position.

Our desperate efforts to pull the obelisk out of its
40° position included building an A-frame, but running out
of time and money, we finally had to accept defeat.

with ropes thrown over the ends. It was difficult to lever from the sides because there was not enough level platform to stand on. The crews strained, the levers bent and some broke, and the sled creaked. But the obelisk would not move.

By this time Ali had attached pulling ropes under the pyramidion and new crews were hauling on them, trying to work in concert with the lever men. But the laws of mechanics were against them. They were pulling from below the slanted obelisk so that their force was directed out and down, and there was no upward component to the pull. Although they were straining mightily they were achieving nothing more than pulling the butt's edge ever more tightly into the turning groove. The obelisk was not tipping up at all.

The day ended in stalemate. We were a week over schedule. We had three hundred workers on the payroll. We were already far over budget and losing money every hour. Mr Hamada's caution – laudable about the sandpit – has crippled us with the ramp. But the happy progress down the ramp to the groove had given us enough heart to risk one more day.

Because of some careless driving on the part of Ali's driver a fight broke out between the local Aswan workmen and those brought in from Luxor. It was not an auspicious start to the day. But Roger attempted to redeem all our effort. He roped together a tall A-frame whose height would change the direction of the pull, giving us an upward component to the force. The hauling hawsers were run over its timber top and laid out for the crews. The frame was lifted into place near the obelisk's pedestal, leaning slightly towards the obelisk. Ali stood to the side and the men took up the strain.

But at the end of a long day in the bleaching, brutal Egyptian sun, our obelisk still reclined at an angle of 40° with a dispirited garland of heavy hawsers and ropes tangled around it. The crews wandered away.

Roger's best efforts had not saved us and, desperately frustrated, he kept insisting that he should have been allowed to follow through with his sandpit idea. We were all peevish and upset. We had, after all, failed.

In the post-mortem discussions we identified mistakes that might have made a critical difference. We should have used the steeper ramp and stronger rock seats for the snubbing timbers. We should have built level platforms on the ramp to allow our lever crews to work from the sides. The crew straining to haul the obelisk upright wasted most of their efforts in pulling the ropes down from an awkward angle; we should have built a causeway on the other side of the obelisk's base to give them a workable angle of pull. We should have used our time more wisely. We should have been supported by the limitless resources of a Pharaoh.

The most sensible and graceful among us was Ali. Sitting in front of the beached obelisk, his long frame eloquent with fatigue, he looked even more like Ramses the Great. He accepted our shortfall philosophically. 'The work goes well. The real problem is, we don't have time.' Mark translated for us, but Ali's hands spoke more fluently than the unfamiliar sibilance of his Arabic. 'How many days and nights have I thought about how to raise the obelisk more quickly? My God, my head was splitting. The men are still enthusiastic, but you just can't do work like this to a deadline.' Later, Mark regained his scholarly distance and attempted to define what the ancient technology was all about. 'Men like Ali with their skill, and the enthusiasm of their men, were probably the most important secret ingredient in all ancient technology.'

We packed our gear and prepared for the journey home. It seemed insane, but we were already thinking of schemes that would bring us back to finish the job. We'd become obsessed with the problem of getting the obelisk up.

We had more in common with the great Unfinished Obelisk of Aswan than we wanted. But this itself was some comfort. We had learned more from the Unfinished Obelisk than from the thirty-odd obelisks around the world. And we had learned more from our failed experiment than archaeologists before us had discovered from academic speculation and paper conjecture.

There were things we could supply, and those we could not. Ali had supplied us with one precious commodity: an inextinguishable willingness to succeed and even exceed. But the old workers were infused with faith, a holy, magical fervour. We were driven by mere curiosity and hampered by book-keeping. We could not supply the generations of trial and error, the intelligent inventiveness, the engineering confidence and the experience. We could only guess at that. And in the end we could not supply that commodity which fascinated the Egyptians more than any other: time.

THE COLOSSEUM

ROBIN BRIGHTWELL

ALMOST two thousand years ago, the Roman Emperor Titus opened the largest, most lavish and most politically influential building of the ancient world – the Colosseum. Built in AD 80, this vast amphitheatre was able to seat a third of the population of Rome and it catered specifically for their taste in entertainment – the mass slaughter of humans and animals.

Thousands of slaves, criminals, prisoners of war and professional combatants – were forced to fight to the death. From dawn to dusk for a hundred days, the slaughter to celebrate the new arena continued. Wildlife was collected from every corner of Titus' empire for the killings. There were elephants from North Africa, hippos from Nubia, elk from Ireland, lions from Mesopotamia, bears, leopards, long-haired buffalo, cheetahs, gazelles, antelope and crocodiles – according to an estimate at the time, five thousand animals were killed on one particular day.

The Colosseum and the events inside it were a gift from Titus to his subjects. He claimed that these free games were to thank them for their past loyalty, but in reality his generosity was to ensure their loyalty in the future. Titus and many other emperors who succeeded him were to learn that the games could guarantee their future, and demonstrate their power and glory. The

The Colosseum in Rome: symbol of power and the site
of mass slaughter.

The Roman Empire when Hadrian became Emperor in AD 117.

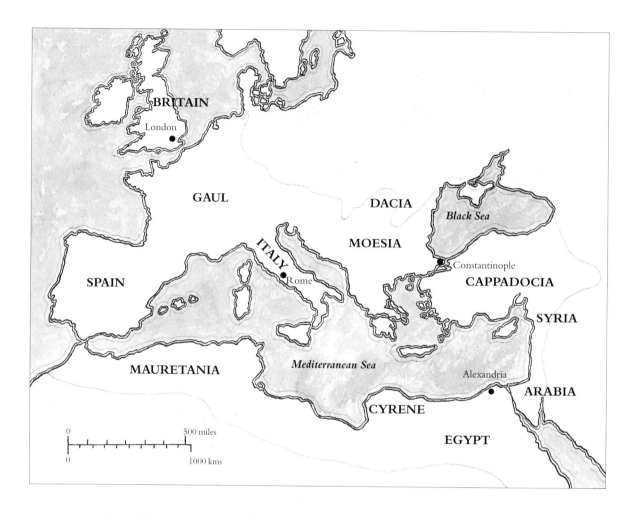

marathon slaughters were to become for Titus a vital reaffirmation of his role as the most powerful man in the world, through which the people's loyalty could be won and maintained. The Roman Empire was a vast territory ruled by one man, and the games became more and more important to maintain his power.

The citizens of Rome had no right to vote, and instead were given what was called 'bread and circuses': food supplies and entertainment. The bloodier the spectacle, the happier the crowd and the more secure the Emperor. Yet the effect of such brutality on the crowd could have been catastrophic: the resultant near hysteria had to be contained and translated into a sense of loyalty to the Emperor

OVERLEAF The magnificent Greek theatre at Ephesus held
as many spectators as modern football stadia.

and the Empire. Of course, this was achieved by the Emperor himself who was present at the games, receiving his subjects' gratitude and adulation.

The range of animals brought to slaughter was only possible because of the vast and growing size of Titus' territories. His Empire stretched from England in the north, to Upper Egypt in the south; and from Morocco and Spain in the west to Armenia and Syria in the east. Imagine being able to travel from Hadrian's Wall, on today's border between England and Scotland, over the Channel to France, south-east across Europe, through the Balkans, right round the eastern Mediterranean, across the top of North Africa as far west as Morocco, cross into Spain and return through France to Britain without passing through any national boundaries.

The Colosseum was opulent in every sense. The seats had been faced in the finest marble, the walls painted gold and purple, and there were beautiful statues in every niche. Yet it had been built in only eight years. The reason for such haste was that it had been commissioned by Titus' father Vespasian, when in his sixties and he was desperate to inaugurate his own magnificent concept. Although he did live to see it virtually finished, he died soon afterwards. It fell to his heir Titus to hold the first events in a building purpose-made to celebrate death.

GREEK TRAGEDY, ROMAN DEBAUCHERY

Although the Roman lust for blood-letting was unprecedented in the history of public performance, the tradition of mass entertainment followed in the footsteps of the Ancient Greeks whose sophisticated plays were written and performed also to very large audiences. The magnificent theatre in Ephesus could seat as many spectators as a modern sports stadium. Plays were the equivalent of television today – mass entertainment rather than something just for intellectuals. The Ephesus building is a wonderful example of Greek design. Large though it is, it still follows the contours of the mountainside on which it was built. Classical Greek drama expressed their myths, and the people's place in the cosmos. The people were part of the natural world, and therefore so was the

theatre. The backdrop to the play was natural too: no scenery was needed because the land or the sea formed the most appropriate setting.

The Romans started to develop their own very different entertainment. The theatres were no longer part of the landscape, but free-standing buildings. The scenery was no longer nature, but a symbolic Roman building, of considerable grandeur. Theatres were becoming vehicles for expressing the Roman Way, as important as State Television in a totalitarian regime of today.

As the conquerors of most of Europe, North Africa and the Middle East, the Romans were determined to shape their own destiny. They were engineers who took on the challenge of any obstacle they faced. They did not go with the grain, but imposed their own solutions. Their roads did not follow the natural contours of the landscape — but were straight. Just to bring water at a consistent gradient into the towns, bridges leapt perilous rivers, valleys were traversed and mountains penetrated. The Romans dictated their own terms and refused to compromise. It was a constant battle for proof of their superiority over nature.

As Roman confidence grew, processing people became almost an art form. Audiences were not simply allowed to pile into buildings. Instead spectators had to enter and exit through external doors where strict order could be maintained.

Greek mass entertainment had frequently included violence and death, but it had always taken place off-stage: the Romans had no such delicacy. It was also a different experience politically. An élite held power in Rome, even in the days of the Republic. As time went by this power was vested in fewer and fewer individuals, culminating in the autocratic rule of the emperors. Roman citizens in audiences were given the illusion of influence, but they were merely spectators and the best they could hope for was that holding out their thumbs really did save a gladiator's life. It was during the struggles between various warlords in the period leading up to the birth of the Roman Empire in 27 BC that large gatherings of spectators were recognized as politically useful tools. Once politicians realized that many people could be manipulated at one time, the way was open to develop the fully fledged games.

The Colosseum had a number of forerunners. The theatre of the great soldier Pompey was built in 55 BC as the first permanent building of this kind in Rome. Pompey was one of three rulers of Rome in the turbulent times just before the first Emperor. He ruled with Julius Caesar and, like him, was murdered. But before his untimely death he showed how the masses could be manipulated by spectacular displays. First he got around the rules against erecting permanent theatres, which were perceived as a potential danger to public order and open to political abuse, by building above a temple dedicated to Venus. Then, on his return to Rome after military victories abroad, he inaugurated it with a dazzling display of 600 mules, 410 leopards and other large cats, 20 elephants and a troupe of monkeys. The people also saw a northern European lynx for the first time, and from the other end of Pompey's territorial conquests, a rhinoceros.

The returning warrior was determined to put on a spectacle so incredible that it would outclass any display by his predecessors or his contemporary rivals. None of the audience would have ever seen most of the poor animals on display: it showed just how powerful Pompey was to be able to bring such wonders home. The event was a clever piece of propaganda, stage-managed to glorify him in the public imagination. By providing a convenient site Pompey could appear before a huge crowd to display and validate his authority. For Pompey himself it was just as appealing to know that his name could live on forever in a permanent shrine to his achievements. Politically it was a triumph.

The Roman statesmen now made a U-turn in their attitude to permanent theatres. Large audiences, which had hitherto been feared as dangerous, were now seen as desirable by men who knew how to exploit them. Ambitious politicians could see that to achieve their goals it made sense to use a permanent site and present spectacles to the masses.

WE WHO ARE ABOUT TO DIE...

One such spectacle was the tradition of gladiatorial combats. Initially fights to the death took place at the funeral of an important figure, or as a memorial to him. The Romans claimed to be calling here on Etruscan tradition, in which such fights took place during the funerals of rich or powerful leaders. At a funeral

Gladiators in action on a Roman mosaic, now in the
Galleria Borghese in Rome. At the time of Julius Caesar 320 pairs of
gladiators fought to the death in one single programme.

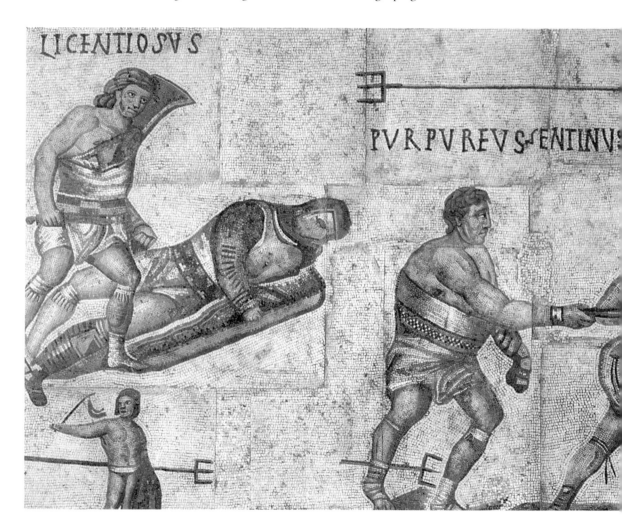

the aim was to put the gods in a good mood to receive the dead chieftain by sacrificing a human being in combat. This does not explain why the gladiatorial
combats became mass entertainment in the way that they did; there must have
been a taste for violence and death, and perhaps the authorities used historical
precedent to justify the unjustifiable. These gladiatorial events also helped to
solve the growing problem of how to deal with captured prisoners of war, since
there were no prisoner-of-war camps. Rather gladiatorial schools were set up
where captured men were trained to fight in the costume and style of their native

country and to provide a diversion in the otherwise humdrum routine of daily life. Later on wellborn Romans, especially penniless young bloods or adventurous men and even women who wanted quick fame and glory, entered the arena to participate in the games.

In Rome gladiators became big business. In the time of Julius Caesar, 320 pairs of gladiators fought in a single programme of events. Matters became worse once the Colosseum had been built: in just eight years, between AD 106 and 114, some 23 000 individuals fought for their lives. As well as prisoners of war, they included condemned criminals and those at the bottom of the social heap. Contractors trained the doomed men and provided bands of gladiators who would fight to the death when the time came, and the crowd required it.

Even though they were at the same level in the Roman social scale as pimps and prostitutes, gladiators were still expected to keep to a strict code. They were trained to fight hard, and to hold to the traditions of bravery that Roman soldiers showed on the battlefield. This was fortunate for the successful fighters, because it meant that there was considerable glory to be had for honourable victory. They could never rise up in society, but they could become idols of the crowd and be copied in children's games, and some of them set women's hearts aflame. They appear in mosaics with small heads and enormous shoulders.

This type of fighter was often a retiarius who fought with a net and trident against a better protected gladiator with a shield and sword. Fighting almost naked, retiarii were no doubt more attractive, but they were prone to frequent non-fatal wounds, which made them slow, and therefore less exciting to watch in combat. Those who were fully armoured were protected from minor wounds, but when their adversary's sword did get through it was often fatal. Such fights were fast and furious until the end. Gladiators were expected to be silent when wounded, and to die nobly. Defeated gladiators, lying on the ground awaiting the death blow, were allowed to ask for mercy from the most powerful man present by holding up a finger. There is a carving showing one in just this situation, as his adversary is about to wield the sword. Just in time, a powerful hand is held out in blessing and he is spared. The death blow, averted in this combat, would have been carried out as quickly and as humanely as possible. That too was part of the training. And it could well be death at the hand of a friend, because gladiators trained together, and were then expected to kill one another in the arena. Although gladiators lived and fought in the hope of life, freedom and glory, an early death was much more likely and only a very few became rich and lived to an old age. Most were forced into their profession because they could find no other way to earn a living. It is difficult for us now to imagine a society which cultivated such bizarre, cruel, but still sophisticated traditions.

THE INTELLECTUAL CONSCIENCE

The pattern of an average day at the arena was that beasts and criminals were killed in the morning and gladiators fought in the afternoon. It was a clever mix. The wild animals provided variety, and could even be set against prisoners condemned to death *ad bestias.* In this way any man or woman who did not worship the Emperor as God might die. At the day's end, the sand would be raked, and the mob would return home satiated, but manipulated, to look forward to tomorrow's show.

The brutalizing of the Romans by day after day of slaughter was all done for sound political reasons. But in Rome there lived writers with high moral standards – why did so few of them condemn it? Everyone went to the games, regardless of sensitivity or sensibility, even the most sophisticated writers of the time. It is difficult today for many northern Europeans to understand even how modern Spanish poets can glorify the events and heroes of the bullring, but a lot more difficult to understand a midweek visit by writers and social commentators such as Pliny, Martial or Suetonius to see a few humans eaten by lions. But go they did.

Often the spectacles were re-enactments of religious stories and myths. Martial describes a bizarre animal event which involved a pregnant sow, and was connected with the story of the birth of Bacchus, the god of wine. He had been conceived when the great god Zeus appeared to Bacchus' future mother, Semele, in mortal form. But when she was pregnant she was tricked by a jealous rival into asking Zeus to come to her in his full and powerful form. As a result she was burned to a crisp, because she was a mere mortal. Zeus took the foetus she was bearing and sewed it into his thigh until it came to term. When this story was portrayed in the arena, Martial wrote: 'When a pregnant sow was struck by a spear, one of the piglets was born from the wound, like Bacchus from poor Semele. When the piglet was born from its sow mother, it ran away.'

Only a few writers expressed views about the events they saw. One of them, Seneca, presents his views as an imaginary conversation between himself and a spectator:

'*Death is the fighter's only exit.*'
'*But this, that or the other fellow has committed highway robbery!*'
'*Well?*'
'*And murder!*'
'*The lash forces them on to the sword.*'
'*Let them have at each other in the nude – get in at the bare chest!*'

There's an interval in the display:

'*Cut a few throats meanwhile to keep things going!*'
'*Come now, can't you people see even this much – that bad examples recoil on those who set them?*'

His description of the crowd chimes with the behaviour of a modern audience watching a violent sport like boxing. We find it easy to condemn another culture but our own still shows some of the same tendencies.

Two thousand years ago it was not the games' cruelty which gave rise to criticism; rather, their bad effects on the citizens. Here is Seneca again:

Nothing is so damaging to good character than the habit of wasting time at the Games; for then it is that vice steals on you through the avenue of pleasure. I come home more greedy, more ambitious, more voluptuous, even more cruel and more inhumane.

Several hundred years later St Augustine wrote of one of his followers, a Christian called Alypius:

When he saw the blood, it was as though he had drunk a deep draught of savage passion. Instead of turning away he fixed his eyes upon the scene and drank in all its frenzy, unaware of what he was doing....He watched and cheered and grew hot with excitement, and when he left the arena, he carried away with him a diseased mind which would leave him no peace until he came back again.

So the games were not only morally corrupting, but addictive. No wonder they worked so well for the politicians' needs!

SYMBOL OF EMPIRE

In the first century BC, a thousand years after the founding of Rome, the first
Emperor was created and replaced the previous triumvirate of rulers. From
27 BC Augustus reigned supreme at the top of a clearly defined social hierarchy,
with slaves at the bottom. The structure of society was formally mirrored in the
amphitheatres of Rome. Under Augustus the seating arrangements were formal-
ized in minute terms in a code of laws known as *Lex Julia Theatralis*. Under these
regulations, audiences in the arenas were arranged according to their social and
legal status. His system was a symbol of the Emperor's strength, carefully designed
to provide the setting for an ordered image of the Roman state. Everybody had
his or her designated place, from the Emperor on the amphitheatre podium to
the women, slaves and foreigners up 'in the gods'. The stage was set for the
exploitation of amphitheatres and particularly the Colosseum, as the manifesta-
tion of the Roman Empire itself.

The Emperor who conceived the Colosseum was Vespasian, a successful
military commander who was the son of a tax collector and frugal himself.
Once he became Emperor in AD 69, he brought stability and a measure of fair
appointments to positions of power. He would have been well-known to the
British of the time as he had led the campaign to subdue them. He took over the
most powerful position the world had ever known just a year after the hugely
unpopular Emperor Nero had committed suicide.

The chosen construction site – perhaps to bury Nero's memory – was a
lake in his private pleasure gardens which had been built right in the centre of
overcrowded Rome. Vespasian was determined to replace the image of his prede-
cessor's excess and self-indulgence by providing something wonderful for
the people on the site. The lake water had to be drained into the Tiber before
building could commence. In the early days of the Colosseum the low-lying
arena could easily be refilled for the staging of mock naval battles. Later this space
was roofed in, and under the arena were built elaborate cages, elevators and
ramps which held and moved exotic animals and humans, participants in the
performances.

THE CONCRETE REVOLUTION

The Colosseum was to be a mammoth piece of construction. The outer ellipse would measure 512 metres. It would be as big as three medieval cathedrals the size of Salisbury Cathedral in southern England and similar in size to the modern Astrodome Stadium in Houston, Texas, which like the Colosseum seats about 45 000 people. Such an ambitious project would involve more stone than even the Empire's vast resources could get cut and dressed in sufficient quantities. The Roman architects needed another building technique, and they found the solution much closer to home.

Near the town of Pompeii, later to be devastated by the eruption of the volcano Vesuvius, a revolutionary discovery was beginning to make its mark. It was to change forever the way in which we build. Sand made by erosion of the volcanic lava, known as *pozzolana,* turned out to have an amazing quality. When mixed with lime, water and gravel it became a substance which we now know as concrete. Roman concrete was quicker and cheaper to use than any other building material of the times, and it was just as tough as its modern equivalent. In addition, fewer skilled workers were required. Arches which had been made out of carefully prepared cut stone could now be thrown up in a fraction of the time. Concrete was therefore the ideal building material for the Romans' immense structures.

The Greeks had concrete too, but because they had relied on air to harden it the inside of one of their large concrete structures could take years to set. Even today samples of their concrete can be found which are still soft inside. Concrete made with the Romans' *pozzolana* sand was set with water rather than air and, more importantly, it became waterproof. It was this quality which gave the Romans the ability to build their famous harbours, aqueducts and bridges.

Archaeologists call it 'the concrete revolution', and it was to have a particularly revolutionary effect in roof-building. Before concrete, the methods used for constructing roofs were limited. One way was to use a flat beam on top of two columns, but this limited the span: the beam would break if it was more than about 8 metres long. Even a complicated timber beam truss, as in Westminster

Hall, can span only 20 metres. Arches have a wider span, but the outward thrust could potentially split a building. Concrete enabled the building technique known as vaulting to be exploited which combined the advantages of the beam and the arch.

Concrete was to prove easier to handle than stone: the workers could pull it up in small, liftable quantities rather than hoisting huge lumps of stone; and its structural advantage is simply that it is easier to shape. But the Colosseum, like most other Roman buildings, shunned concrete as a material to be seen and celebrated: it was used only for the supporting structural skeleton which was then fleshed out with more attractive materials. The passages and vaults were all made with concrete cores – 6000 tonnes of concrete in all – but they were faced with stone. And although the eighty interior radiating walls supporting the marble seats were made of brick-faced rubble concrete, the amphitheatre walls were constructed of travertine, a decorative limestone which was quarried near Tivoli.

THE INVISIBLE ROOF

The oval shape of the Colosseum focused every spectator on the entertainment itself. Just as in our cinemas today, the outside world with all its problems was invisible. Control of the audience even extended to getting them in and out, with an efficiency which would be the envy of a football stadium designer of the twentieth century. The first three storeys were each composed of eighty arches. At ground level they were numbered, leading people to carefully segmented rows within the building. These eighty arches (known as vomitoria) worked so efficiently with their numbered staircases that a full audience of 45 000 could leave the building in ten minutes flat.

The games would draw the crowd to the Colosseum, but how to keep them there in comfort? The games lasted from morning to night and the heat must have been overpowering. Even today, southern Europe shuts down at lunchtime for several hours because it is so hot: anyone who has sat out in the noonday sun in the Mediterranean summer knows how unbearable it is. The solution to avoid interrupting the spectacle in an amphitheatre, would surely be a roof.

There is no trace of a roof in the Colosseum today; nor are there any archaeological remains. In fact there is no sign of a roof on any one of the remaining seventy-five amphitheatres scattered across what used to be the Roman Empire. So was there a roof or not? The answer is to be found in the poetry of ancient Rome. One writer, Dio Cassius, mentions an amphitheatre cover on the 'golden day' when Nero had the whole stage and all the actors covered in gold, and there were 'awnings high to keep out the sunshine, coloured purple with gold stars surrounding the picture of Nero on a golden chariot'. Inscriptions on walls, the Roman equivalent of advertising hoardings, state that 'there will be killing of animals and there will be awnings' or 'awnings, gladiators, killing of animals and a special attraction: crucifying criminals'.

In his famous book on architecture, Vitruvius describes how before the performance could begin 'the audience had to be seated, the awnings spread out, and the machinery put in place'. The poet Lucretius writes of trembling and fluttering awnings over earlier theatres spread out from posts and beams and bathing the assembled audience with yellow, red and purple in a 'laughing flood of beauty when the light of day is thus confined'. Pliny writes that Julius Caesar stretched awnings over the entire Forum along the Sacred Way up to the Capitoline Hill, a sight 'more wonderful than the show of gladiators'.

This written evidence describes the roofs as being temporary, flexible giant coverings over the banks of seats. For a big amphitheatre such a roof would have been as big as one of the modern roofs over massive football and Olympic stadia, yet they were made from the crude materials and with the technology of two thousand years ago. The secrets of their construction were lost when the Empire collapsed because none of the methods was ever recorded. To help us understand how it may have been done, we decided that our building project would be to try to re-create a giant awning, but before we started we wanted to find out why the Romans did not use their magic, newly discovered material to build a permanent roof.

WHY NOT CONCRETE?

Perhaps the greatest achievement in concrete that the Romans ever pulled off was the giant domed roof of the Pantheon. It was started in 27 BC but owes its present appearance to the Emperor Hadrian, who restored it over a hundred years later. It remained the largest permanent unsupported roof in the world until the twentieth century. The wide dome was built with several different types of concrete. The mix was graded, with heavy gravel aggregate at the bottom and lightweight materials at the top. The heavier concrete is stronger, but the higher up the dome the Romans built, the less strength was needed. At the very top the round window opening is surrounded by concrete made with pumice – volcanic ash. Pumice is light enough to float on water, so the top of the dome is made of the lightest concrete possible. This roof is Rome's biggest one in concrete, but it is only 43.3 metres wide; the Colosseum is 189 metres at its widest!

The engineer who was to apply his expertise to our roof building project, Chris Wise, works for Ove Arup, the company which engineered the Sydney Opera House, which opened in 1973. Ever since then the company has had a reputation for constructing beautiful, but well-nigh impossible buildings. At thirty-six years old, Chris is one of their senior engineers who has built what they call 'lightweight' roofs. These are the giant structures made from modern plastic, metal and carbon fibre that cover football and Olympic stadia. He is therefore an expert in spanning big spaces and understands the theory of holding things up in the air better than almost anyone else in Britain. He was the ideal person to decide whether a concrete roof spanning the Colosseum would have been possible.

A beam construction would have been out of the question, he said, because the number and width of the supporting columns for the beams would have completely obscured the view of every spectator. A dome could in theory have been built. However, to provide enough support, it would have not only spanned the current building, but would have had to extend many metres outside it. The building would have looked like an upturned bowl, and the thickness of the concrete at the level of the top of the current walls would have been 25 metres!

LEFT The famous concrete, domed roof of the Pantheon in Rome.
RIGHT The modern roof of the Italian World Cup stadium in Bari.

Even if the Romans could have borne the sight of such a giant saucer, they would have baulked at the sheer quantity of concrete. They had no choice but to make a lightweight roof.

ASSESSING THE EVIDENCE

Roman tent roofs are no longer around for us to see and what little evidence is left today is obscure, so it is not surprising that most people have never even heard of them. They are surrounded by mystery – how were they put up and how did they stay up? These roofs were unprecedented structures, so how did the

Romans even get the idea to build them? Chris Wise is in the vanguard of modern designers who have recently begun to match the Romans' achievements, but only by using new materials. He was an ideal engineer to try to repeat the ancients' achievement.

The literary evidence had told us that the awnings existed, but gave Chris no idea how to construct them. For this he needed other types of evidence. Ammianus Marcellinus, a fourth-century historian, reports that the awnings originated in the coastal cities of southern Italy, and a famous wall painting discovered in 1896 substantiates this. It depicts a brawl between the Pompeiians and their neighbours in AD 59. The fight occurred in the double-staircased amphitheatre in Pompeii, and the painting shows the structure partially covered by what appears to be an immense awning extending over half the enclosure. This drape-like awning is either supported by, or extended to, the towers along the city walls. The awning itself hangs in curves between ropes or beams supported from some undisclosed area behind or along the uppermost storey of the building. An additional rope on the right is shown extending down to the ground. The perspective in this Pompeiian painting is obviously naive: the awning is lifted to the sky to enable the viewer to see the brawl clearly. Consequently what supported the awning was hidden from view.

Vela (singular *velum*) was the Latin name given to these tent roofs throughout the Empire. Even Greek theatres, which did not originally have roofing, received the canvas roof treatment under Roman rule. *Vela* served as sunshades only; they offered no protection against the rain. The material was dyed different colours and occasionally richly decorated. The provinces could not always afford them, so their rare appearances must have provoked great excitement.

The evidence of the Pompeiian painting was a start in Chris Wise's design process, but was too vague to be of much help. It then turned out that some amphitheatres themselves contain clues, high up on their walls. At Nîmes in the south of France is the best-preserved Roman amphitheatre in the world. Here is physical evidence for the existence of the awnings and part of the means by which they were supported. Just below the perimeter of the upper wall around the entire building are the remains of stone brackets which project from the walls

Evidence for the existence of awnings – a wall painting at
Pompeii and the amphitheatre at Nîmes. On the upper level at
Nîmes, the holes in the corbels are clearly visible.

and are arranged in pairs, one above the other. The top bracket, or corbel, has a hole in the middle; the lower one is cup-shaped and sits a couple of metres below. They could easily have been used to support a mast, and Roman coins clearly show masts along the cornice of the Colosseum itself. The lower stone would have cradled the bottom of the mast while the upper stone kept it vertically against the wall.

But how do we know that the masts were not just for flags or banners to advertise the games or the Emperor's presence? Simply because the size of the holes in the corbels is too great for even an Emperor-size flagpole. At the Colosseum itself enough corbels remain to work out that there would have been 240 masts spaced about 2 metres apart, surely far too many just to hold flags? Once Chris Wise knew that there had been masts, it was obvious to him that some form of rope network could be constructed within the arena and held up by the masts. But were masts, rope and canvas sufficient, or were other elements involved?

SPECULATION

Our team was by no means the first group to try to solve the awning problem. During the late Renaissance a huge interest developed in all things Roman. A number of illustrations and theses appeared which speculated on how the awnings must have looked and how they were used. In 1682 the French architectural historian Antoine Desgaodetz published an elaborate study of the Colosseum: he thought that the awning covered the entire amphitheatre and was a protection against sun and rain. In 1725 this was refuted by Carlo Fontana, who proposed that the covering had a central opening: a circle or ellipse, perhaps of rope, suspended above the arena by ropes from the masts. These ropes supported the awning, obviously with a central hole in it. The hole was above the area where the actual slaughter took place – no one down there would be too concerned about a bad case of sunstroke. In Fontana's engraving, the awning seems to consist of one enormous piece of cloth made up of pie-shaped sections permanently sewn together and held by ropes tied directly to the masts.

In 1848 Luigi Canina proposed a solution using a series of stone bollards set at ground level around the outside of the Colosseum. There is good evidence for these: some still exist around the remains. If these stones had been fitted with windlasses or winches, they could have helped in the raising of the roof. Modern students of the Colosseum have also drawn on the stones for a solution. Alberto Carpiceci, author of a popular guidebook to Rome, describes as one of his ideas the roof as a trellis made of wood or metal. The virtue of such a rigid structure, to his mind, is that it would have prevented the central form being pulled out of shape by uneven traction. The raising of the ropes would have been done by more than a hundred men pulling rhythmically from outside the Colosseum on ground level at the bollards. Once the ropes had been raised to the desired height, they would then be tied off to the masts at the top of the building, eliminating the danger of vandalism.

GATHERING EVIDENCE

All these ideas were pure speculation, and none had been tested. What is more, such writers did not have any practical experience or knowledge of flexible roofs. It fitted the pattern that we had discovered in researching each programme in the series. Those who have the interest in the secrets of lost empires and the skills to find and interpret the evidence are historians and archaeologists who have seldom wielded a hammer, let alone shaped a stone or tried to build an arch. It was only when we involved an appropriate range of practical experts that the realistic possibilities and problems became clear. The field was therefore open for Chris Wise to test the best and most accurate of the ideas. But it is all too easy to leap to conclusions about how something might have been done; to begin with he needed to consult the best available expert on historical accuracy. For the Roman awnings there was no question who to choose: architectural historian Rainer Graefe is the only expert in this obscure subject.

After training as a historian, Graefe found a job with the foremost designer of lightweight roofs in Germany, Frei Otto. It was while he was studying in

Stuttgart that he stumbled across a reference to the *vela*. Two years into his PhD, he abandoned it and threw himself with passion into examining this ancient phenomenon. His quest took him all over the Roman Empire, recording the architectural evidence and photographing almost every major amphitheatre still in existence. The culmination of his work was the publishing of a book called *Vela Erunt* (*There Will Be Vela*) after a graffiti inscription found at Pompeii. His theory about how they were made differed drastically from anybody else's. Rainer has complete faith in his own historical analysis, which is what we chose him for, and he dislikes any scheme for roof building which goes against the conclusions he has reached following seven years of painstaking research. But until our project his ideas had never been tested. He would be bound to disagree if anyone was to come up with a scheme which worked, but for which there was no historical evidence. And that was exactly what was to happen.

Rainer decided that the Romans would have built the skeleton out of timber. His design consisted of vertical masts, which rose above the outer wall at regular intervals; and then horizontal poles or booms projecting into the interior space and suspended by rope from the masts. The booms jutted out above the rows of seats. Attached to these booms was the tent roof made of individual sections arranged side by side. The awning was suspended by rings from the booms which would have been made so that the rings could slide to and fro. This detail was important since lightweight roofs are sensitive to wind. A mere breeze could cause the canvas to flutter and flap so a smoothly working furling system to protect the awning from ripping was essential. The whole tent roof had to be retractable right to the back of the amphitheatre wall.

Rainer knew that they had achieved these features because of a contemporary anecdote about the perverted Emperor Caligula's cruelty to an amphitheatre audience: he had the awning drawn back during the hottest part of the day and forbade anyone to leave. Also the Roman satirist Martial, describing a juggler who never misses a catch, says that he is faultless even when 'rushing winds tear at the awning which cannot be spread' – a clear indication that the awning could be extended or drawn back on windy days. Certainly on a suspended tent roof the wind could cause enormous damage.

Across from the Colosseum is another piece of evidence that Rainer used – a stone identified earlier this century as a device for determining wind direction. The names of the winds are inscribed on it. In its centre is a hole which would have held an upright dowel; streamers would have blown from it, showing the direction of the wind and giving an idea of its strength by how horizontal they were. Because of the need to draw the awning back, Rainer concluded, the material between the booms would not have been fitted tightly between them but would have sagged when fully hoisted out. This conclusion comes from simple geometry: the further into the middle of a circle, the smaller the circumference becomes. This could explain the hanging folds of the *vela* in the Pompeii wall painting.

Chris Wise, our engineer from Ove Arup, found Rainer Graefe's theory based on a wooden skeleton unconvincing. The combination of masts, poles, ropes and canvas would, Chris thought, have 'collapsed under its own weight'. He was more attracted to the old theories which proposed a rope web suspended from the circle of masts, with each rope joined at its inner end to a rope circle. When the ropes were tightened at each mast, the tension would have raised the web of ropes in the arena, and the canvas could then be suspended from them. Chris thought that this was a more practical and elegant solution for covering the amphitheatre. Elegant it may have been to a London-based engineer, but it could not be furled quickly, like a sail, and that was to turn out to be its Achilles heel. Chris agreed that the fairest approach would be to test both methods – his rope web and Rainer's boom system – and he set to work on his computer to organize the details.

THE RIGGERS

One look at the Colosseum and it is obvious that, whether the cover was suspended from Rainer's horizontal booms or Chris's cobweb of ropes, the awning would have involved a massive quantity of timber, ropes and cloth. It would have needed great skill and experience to rig, control and derig it,

Roman sailors in the rigging of their boat, from a
tomb decoration at Pompeii. Sailors probably erected
awnings over the Colosseum.

especially if the wind suddenly increased in strength. This would have had to be
done quickly, with 45 000 excited spectators sitting under it, not to mention a
few hungry lions in the middle of the arena. Who would have had the skills?

Not long ago a gas main was being put in close to the Colosseum and the
workers discovered the remains of a sailors' barracks. Since Rome is many miles
from the sea, the sailors must have been doing something which did not involve
ships. And the remains made it clear that these were sailors based a long way
down the coast, close to modern Naples. More evidence that sailors worked the
awnings comes from Lampridius, a fourth-century historian. He writes of the
mad Emperor Commodus who repeatedly fought in the arena as a gladiator.
Once, when some members of the audience howled and applauded, Commodus

was enraged because he thought that they were making fun of him: he had the offenders brought down into the arena and 'put to death by the sailors who worked the awning'. Two more facts to complete the connections between awnings and sails: awnings were made of a linen-like fabric called carbasina – the same cloth that was used by shipbuilders for sails; and the original meaning of *vela* was 'sails'.

If the Romans used nautical knowhow Chris Wise felt he would be advised to do the same, so Owain Roberts, a nautical archaeologist from the University of Wales in Bangor, was brought in to help him. Owain used to be a school-teacher, but his hobby took over, and he now works at the University of Wales as a sailing historian. In 1985 he had helped make a lifesize ancient sail for a recon-structed Greek sailing vessel known as a trireme, so his knowledge of ropes, sails and rigging proved invaluable. His practical knowledge turned out to be even more useful. For Owain, Rainer's awning was simply a question of turning a Roman ship's sail on its side.

Apart from the shortage of evidence, and with nothing in existence to copy, the very basis of constructing the roof was a mystery. For Rainer's beam system, how was the horizontal pole attached to the mast? For the rope cobweb favoured by Chris, how was the rigging for the rope circle in the middle raised? If it was being raised from the top of the ring of masts round the amphitheatre, would there have been enough tension and force to pull it up and lash it? Would the mast be strong enough not to bend or break? Would there have been enough space on the top of an amphitheatre wall to haul in the rope? And as for the awning itself, how was it put up? A ship's sail falls by gravity, but in the amphithe-atre there would only be a slight slope to the centre and not enough to cause the awning to fall by its own weight. Was it extended manually by sailors, or would a pulley system have existed at the centre, like laundry lines let out over a courtyard from one apartment to another?

Rainer's timber boom option certainly had the advantage that everything did not have to depend on everything else, as in a cobweb of ropes. However, it relied on the more complicated horizontal poles which had no place in Chris's rope option. Our aim was to find out which was the better method.

We had learned while rebuilding Stonehenge that engineers are skilled at designing structures which work, but are not so hot at actually building them. So to help Chris put up these two roofs we brought in another specialist, Brian Austen.

Brian is a successful entrepreneur whose company erects stands and seating at major functions in London's Hyde Park, at Ascot races, for the Grand National and for circus big tops. A partner of the circus owner Gerry Cottle, Brian is a self-made man who learned his business the hard way. At the age of sixteen he ran away from home to join the circus. After years of performing, including trapeze work and lion taming – a sport, incidentally, which has its origins in the Colosseum where animal tamers used to entertain the crowds between killings – he set up his own business supplying and erecting circus tents. He is impressively practical, having rebuilt a helicopter from an old shell, and is getting a pilot's licence so that he can test it out. He deals frequently with masts up to 18 metres long, and with the problems of tensioning long ropes over large areas. Brian's natural technical ability and instinct for solving problems rescued our construction attempts from a lot of inevitable practical difficulties.

THE SEARCH FOR A SUITABLE SITE

Before we could begin to build a roof, this team of engineer, historian, sailor and circus tent erector had to have access to an amphitheatre over which they could build it. Naturally no official responsible for a Roman monument was going to allow them to turn a priceless archaeological treasure into a building site. Even if they had, no amphitheatre is preserved well enough to make the construction possible.

An alternative had to be found, and Xanten in north-west Germany looked like the answer. As the only large Roman city north of the Alps which was not built over after the collapse of the Roman Empire, it became a treasure trove for archaeologists. In the 1970s there was a proposal to build an industrial estate over it. Then, in return for sparing the site, the authorities insisted that the excavations be given popular appeal. So instead of merely uncovering ground plans, full-blown reproductions of the main buildings in the ancient town were made. The amphitheatre had been almost totally reconstructed and it seemed the ideal site over which to build the awnings. But there was a crucial problem: at an outdoor venue in northern Germany it was unlikely that the sun would have been too hot for comfort, so an awning would not have been necessary. Not surprisingly, this amphitheatre lacked one essential component – the stone brackets or corbels to hold the masts. While the authorities in Xanten were now keen on the idea of incorporating corbels into their amphitheatre, they insisted that they should be built with the same materials and to the same high standards as the rest of the building. The idea was good but the cost astronomical. Just to put the corbels in would have swallowed the whole budget and more besides. Back to square one.

In the end the solution seemed obvious. The project would be carried out on a site that most closely resembled an amphitheatre, both in its structure and in what went on inside. The nearest modern equivalent of the Roman amphitheatre is the Spanish bullring. Bullfighting is still at the centre of popular traditional culture in Spain. The bulls are baited for public amusement and the bullfighters are revered as heroes. This so-called dance of death is as carefully stage-managed for impact as the Roman games were two thousand years ago. The gladiators, like the matadors today, were idolized. Young Roman children would play gladiators, and the more impassioned ladies would lust after and occasionally even elope with them. And there was another reason to cover the arena: the hot weather in Spain creates the need for shade. Even at four in the afternoon you pay more for bullring seats in the shade.

STARTING TO RECONSTRUCT THE VELUM

In April 1995 the group of experts with film crew, support staff and labourers in tow, finally arrived at the bullring that was to become an intensive worksite for the two-week project. The chosen ring was less than half the size of the

The aqueduct at Merida – one of the most
sophisticated and well-preserved of Roman cities – was
possibly used to carry water into the amphitheatre.

Colosseum and, in common with other bullrings, had a lot less seating relative to
arena than there would have been in the Roman amphitheatres. Barcarrota was
the name of the small, remote village in southern Spain which housed this beautiful ring. The walls of the bullring were formed from part of a fifteenth-century
Moorish castle and included a belltower which played home to a couple of
nesting storks.

The other great advantage of Barcarrota was its proximity to Merida, one of
Europe's best-kept secrets for scholars and enthusiasts of Ancient Rome. The
Roman bridge which brings you into the new town has only recently been
closed to traffic and the Roman theatre is one of the best preserved in the world.
Norma Goldman, an American expert in ancient fabrics who was asked to give
guidance on the historical context for our film, describes it as possessing the
almost perfect 'municipal kit'. Wherever they went, the Romans created mini-
Romes: they built amphitheatres like the Colosseum and tried to re-create a

Roman lifestyle no matter how far away they were from the capital – and Merida was one of the most westerly outposts of the Empire.

The Romans became adept at building lifelines to connect their communities and supply them with the means for survival. Merida had two reservoirs as well as aqueducts and a maze of undergound conduits to bring fresh water tapped from underground streams. The precious water fed private and public baths, where people came to socialize and exercise as well as to clean themselves. Merida has one of the few remaining functioning Roman baths. Unfortunately for seventy-three-year-old Norma, who gallantly agreed to be filmed in it, it was not, like many of the original Roman baths, heated!

The preparations for the project had started long before we arrived at Barcarrota. First, the corbels had to be attached to the walls (the Romans would have incorporated their corbels as they were building up the walls). Our corbels were made of metal but had the same carrying capacity as the old stone equivalents. The bottom corbel had to be more firmly anchored to the wall than the rest because the weight of the vertical timber mast would go straight down through it. There was also a very real danger that the load of the awning pulling inwards could kick the mast outwards and pull out the lower corbel.

The Romans had already faced such a problem at their amphitheatre in Nîmes, where one corbel had been broken and an additional hole then made in which to insert the mast. This is not surprising, because this part of France endures gusts of wind of up to 100 mph when the Mistral blows. Theory dictates that the carrying capacity of the masts would be increased if the corbels were as far apart above each other as possible, but at Nîmes the Roman builders decreased the carrying capacity by spacing the two corbels only about 2 metres above one another, rather than the usual 3½–5 metres. Then they strengthened the masts by adding iron rings to fix them to the corbels. It is a puzzle, because on the one hand they were designing for less force on the masts, and then they seem to have realized their mistake and added the metal brackets to try to reinforce the structure in order to cope with the Mistral. Perhaps the Nîmes amphitheatre was not originally designed to carry awnings and so they had to compromise.

THE BOOM AWNING

At the Barcarrota bullring the first task was to attempt to construct Rainer Graefe's boom-based awning, and the first step was to put up the vertical masts from which all his booms, ropes and canvas would eventually hang, if all went well. Chris calculated, or rather his computer did, that a 7.2-metre-high mast would be big enough for the job. He even designed a crane to hoist up the mast. Cranes to winch up objects were commonplace on Roman building sites, although wheelbarrows had still not been invented, and our engineer thought that he had come up with one which was consistent with Roman capabilities. He set aside a morning to make it.

Meanwhile Brian, the circus tent builder, came up with an altogether neater solution. He lashed three large pieces of wood together and within twenty minutes had made a crane which could have worked at any time in the history of human building projects. It was shaped like a wigwam with a 12-metre-long piece of wood acting as the projecting neck of the crane. The idea was to put the crane at the top of the bullring wall, hang a rope with a pulley over the wall, pick up the mast horizontally from the ground below, tip it up vertically when it got to the top and slot it into the corbel. It turned out to be our first proof that it had been right to bring along practical men as well as theoreticians.

Brian was certainly no novice to this task: he uses two poles lashed together in an A-shape to erect main big-top masts. These are up to 25 metres tall – three times longer than the awning's mast. Our mast weighed 500 kg and Brian designed a pulley system to keep the numbers of human pullers down to a minimum. Once the mast was up, its function would be to support the horizontal boom and in this way to carry the full load of a section of roof.

When we raised the mast, the crucial part of the manoeuvre was to turn it to a vertical position. As it was raised to its full height there was a loud cracking noise. The mast and ropes were being wedged up against the side of the wall, creating a lot of friction. With the mast being pulled both ways, the weight on the crane was about to break it. There followed several panic-stricken minutes for engineer Chris while some of our workforce tried to poke the mast free from

Evidence of the skills and technology of Roman builders –
a hoist with pulleys on the Roman tomb of the Haterii.

LEFT Workmen carrying a mast to our site, the bullring at Barcarrota.
RIGHT Brian in a bosun's chair works on the base of the first mast.

the wall. Finally, success – the mast was eased into the corbels without further mishap.

Owain explained that the untreated timber was naturally going to crack while under strain and that the Romans would have been well used to these dangerous-sounding noises: they had had over a thousand years of sailing with bending masts. Bending timber is not common today. Owain believed that Chris had stipulated overheavy beams which were not designed to flex. The ancient sailing ship on which he had worked in Greece had a boom, or yard, which Owain thought had been designed with greater historical accuracy; it was meant to bend. Even today in Bangladesh, he said, you can see vessels with single square sails whose yards are almost bent into moon shapes. The absorption of energy by bending is what gives the wood its strength. Owain believes that modern man finds this a difficult concept to grasp, being so used to building with every element rigid.

Once the masts were up, the booms could be suspended from them, and it was these which would carry the awning fabric itself. No one knew how Chris was going to connect the mast to the boom because he had spent months avoiding the issue. In the event Owain came up with the solution. His design was finally revealed on the day of its realization. There was to be no connection at all! The boom was held in tension at both ends from ropes running through the pulley at the top of the mast. The connections were only with rope, and the boom and mast hung independently from each other.

Many of the building stages that caused concern and difficulty for this modern team would have been easy for the Roman sailors. For example, once the mast and boom were joined together with the boom suspended parallel above the outside wall, the whole contraption had to be turned somehow so that the boom was in position over the seats. Would the mast swivel or stay put in its corbel? Would it get twisted? Would it even snap? Sail expert Owain was confident that the mast would twist round with everything else. He was right. The mast twisted and the boom turned its 90° with such ease that everybody was taken by surprise. This manoeuvrabilty meant that all the rigging could be done to the boom easily while it was at working height, rather than 10 metres up above the seating.

Chris Wise had done some sophisticated computer modelling back in London and had worked out that the long heavy boom hanging out over the seats could only be supported by tying the back end of it to the bottom of the mast. This one fixing supported everything, yet no one had worked out how to get to it 6 metres up in the air. Certainly the Romans would have used scaffolding all the time, yet Chris thought it unlikely that they would have scaled the Colosseum walls at 50 metres high. In any case our schedule allowed us no time to bother with scaffolding. In the event Brian came up with the idea of a bosun's chair on which he was hauled up to complete the last important lashings. This final tieback ultimately held the whole roof down.

The next problem was to get the canvas on. To tension the canvas and create the possibility of pulling it back and forth meant attaching ropes to the far end of the boom, now many metres out over the seats. It suddenly dawned on Chris that he should have thought about this before he swung the booms out. No one in the team relished the prospect of venturing out high above the concrete seating, and Brian was no longer around to help since he had to go back to England to set up a tour by the Moscow State Circus. Swinging the booms back again was discounted as impractical because the whole amphitheatre would have had a complete circle of projecting booms, and in order to get just one of them back, they would all have to be turned. The sailors would have found a different way.

Rainer, whose method this was, and who was meant to make sure that we kept a decent standard of historical accuracy, suggested using footropes. These are made by circling the beam with ropes and then threading another rope through them. This system is used all the time by sailors when reefing a sail on a big ship, and in our case it would enable someone to crawl out along the boom. It seemed a good idea. But Owain, as a stickler for nautical detail, waded in with an objection. Footropes were not invented until at least AD 1600, and ancient pictures of Roman rigging show sailors sitting or standing on the wooden yard while taking the rope out. It was not, assured Owain, difficult to do: twenty years younger and he would have gone out himself. Fortunately one of our trusty helpers from London, Mike O'Rorke, volunteered to go out instead. But when he edged out slowly up to the first rope he found he could go no further: the rope was threatening to push him off as he tried to manoeuvre himself around it. His lack of rigging experience meant that he had neither the confidence nor the ability to get out to the end.

The team now thought that they would have to go through the embarrassment of reaching the end of the boom with the aid of a ladder, a method which they knew was impracticable if applied to the much larger Colosseum – 50-metre ladders were unlikely to have existed then. On the verge of giving up, Chris finally realized that the boom could not only swing side to side, but also tilt up and down. He suggested lowering the boom so that its end rested on the seats, where it would be at working height. Rainer, still trying to stick to historical accuracy with academic zeal, immediately objected to this plan. Although the suggestion was sensible for the bullring, he argued that at the Colosseum there simply would not have been the room to do it. Below where the boom juts out

BELOW Mike O'Rorke trying to attach a rope to the beam.
BOTTOM All five beams complete and in position ready for the canvas.

The boom awning complete with canvas.

was a 5-metre-wide covered walkway which would have prevented the booms from reaching the seats. At Nîmes, however, where the seats go up to the back walls, he conceded that such a method would have been possible.

Chris decided to ignore all this annoying historical detail. Whilst manoeuvring the boom into position to lower it, he was again surprised by the flexibility of the roof's design. The boom, he discovered, could be raised in its horizontal position, so that if it had been tilted at the Colosseum it would have stayed clear of the walkway roof. Even the sceptical Rainer came round to agreeing that this versatile system could have been deployed at the Colosseum.

Then the canvas was attached, the booms were raised back to their horizontal position and Owain demonstrated how the furling would work. It was amazingly simple, needing only two people per canvas segment and it could all be operated from the safety of the bullring wall. The beauty of the system was that each segment was totally independent from the next, so no coordination would be necessary to furl and unfurl. The roof was up, and it worked. Rainer was thrilled to see something finally realized which he had spent so long researching.

Chris's big criticism of Rainer's method was that it was not resistant to wind uplift – nothing held the roof down. He was worried about the wind ripping the canvas and taking the entire structure off. Brian, however, did not share his concern, and had been in so many windy circus sites that his opinion was convincing: he argued that because the wind could get equally below and above the horizontal sail there would be no uplift. Also, unlike a sail which is rigged tightly, the sheets were festooned so deeply that there was no chance that they would be tautened or torn by the wind.

Chris had another criticism: he did not believe that the method could be extended to the length needed for the Colosseum, which would have involved making a boom several times longer. He knew that this would only be possible if the timber was much more slender – otherwise the mast could not take the strain. And a boom so slender would surely buckle. Owain pointed out that the amphitheatre booms would have been lashed together in three sections getting progressively lighter so that the bend was mostly at the end. Chris, he said, had relied too much on his computer; he, Owain, was sure that the mast could withstand a lot more force if it were taller and thinner. Chris was not going to take such questioning of his engineering skills and countered that it did not matter how tall the mast was – what mattered was the size of the mast hole. The corbel dictated the size of the mast, which in turn dictated the span of the roof. Varying the height of the mast would only alter the angle of the ropes and not have any effect on the length of the booms.

Whoever was right, there was a major problem with Rainer's theory. Our German expert's roof could not cover the entire Colosseum seating. Even he was happy to acknowledge that. Given that the most important people, including the Emperor, sat at the front, Chris argued that the Romans would not have been happy with an awning that only covered the back rows of seats and not the ones near the front which had the best view of all the exciting events down in the arena. Chris had gradually come round to agreeing with Rainer that the boom method could go out as far as 30 metres, but in the Colosseum even that is still 20 metres short of covering the front. Rainer acknowleged the roof's limits but did not believe that the Romans had the ability to span any further, however much they may have wanted it. In any case, the shape of the amphitheatres meant that there was more seating at the back than the front, so most people were shaded by the awnings even if these fell short. As further proof that the Romans lived happily with their foreshortened awning, Rainer cited the story of Caligula who, one boiling hot day, was so angered by the audience that he ordered the awnings to be drawn back and forbade anyone to leave. Rainer asserted that he would hardly have inflicted this punishment upon himself, and so must have had his own personal awning or sunshade.

THE ROPE AWNING

With one awning successfully erected, designed by the historically accurate Rainer, and having had a full argument over its merits, it was time for construction to stop for a while. Barcarrota was about to celebrate Easter and a filming project was not going to be allowed to get in the way. As well as processions and general merrymaking, the town was planning a bullfight. Posters advertising the event had gone up weeks before. Being close to the border with Portugal, Barcarrota was to host a typical Portuguese bullfight: instead of fighting on foot, the matadors would fight on horseback. The bullring was going to be packed with people.

Whatever personal feelings on the subject were, the bullfight needed to be filmed. But in the end the whole event was cancelled. Despite posters depicting horsemen facing bulls bristling with dangerously long and sharp-looking horns, the excuse was that the matadors had abandoned the challenge because the bulls' horns had not been filed properly!

After Easter the town returned to normal, and it was time to try Chris's simpler way of erecting a Roman awning. Despite Rainer's opinion that there was no historical evidence, Chris believed that his all-rope roof could have been built. The materials were there, as was the expertise to build it. And in principle it could span the entire seating of the Colosseum. Using taller masts a full 12 metres high, Chris suggested slinging a rope from side to side across the arena – rather like a suspension bridge. This rope would be suspended from the top of the masts. Then another rope, attached further down each mast, would hang below. Upper and lower ropes would be connected at intervals by smaller vertical ropes, called droppers, which would bear the weight of the canvas. The main ropes would meet at a rope circle or oculus in the middle, suspended directly above the arena. The advantage of this method is that, by taking the load from one side to the other, more than one mast at a time absorbs the weight of the roof.

Although Brian, the big-top expert, inclined towards Chris's method as the more practical solution for covering the Colosseum, he believed that Rainer's method would be easier to maintain. Both he and Owain agreed that a furling system for the all-rope method would be extremely difficult to rig. And all the evidence pointed to a desperate need for rapid furling if the wind got up. Because of the way Chris envisaged his idea, furling a sail back and forth would be impossible: the small ropes or droppers coming down from the top rope to the bottom would get in the way of pulling the canvas back. Perhaps fortunately for Chris, this part of his design was never tested.

BELOW LEFT Setting out the ropes. BELOW RIGHT Laying out the canvas.
BOTTOM Chris gives instructions as the canvas is raised.

Chris's method required a complete ring of masts around the whole bull-ring. Because of the enormous cost, Chris decided to show the detail of how it would work using just six masts 3.5 metres apart. All the rope had to be measured out carefully, laid out in segments which corresponded to the separate panels of canvas. While our project helpers attached the canvas ready to raise it, ropes were running like spaghetti everywhere and it would not have been difficult to mess the whole system up completely through just one small mistake. Meanwhile, outside anyone's control and after two weeks of hot calm weather, a storm was brewing and a gusty wind was getting up. Chris feared for the canvas.

Bigger and more immediate trouble loomed in Brian's mind. He did not believe that Chris would get the awning up. He knew that the lower rope could not be tightened, and if this was not done the whole structure would be unstable.

As they started to raise the roof, the wind was getting stronger. Chris was prepared for an enormous uplift from it when they started to pull. The roof rose slowly, as the workers pulled. As Brian had predicted, the lower rope, which could not be tensioned, was making the sail go out of shape. The rope was slack and it could not be controlled. The droppers were no longer hanging straight down, but were skewed. The idea of opposing forces – one holding the roof up and one holding it down – went by the board. The canvas was flapping uncontrollably. The rings which held the canvas on to the ropes turned out to be the weakest link in the chain and began to break. The canvas started to rip away from the ropes. Brian rushed to the top in an attempt to try and hold it down, and he managed to get the roof under control by manually tensioning the lower rope. The result was a roof that was less neat and tidy than the previous boom method. Chris blamed the materials rather than his design; he was convinced that, if only more pulleys had been ordered, his roof would have worked perfectly.

THE FINAL VERDICT

Seeing them side by side, Rainer's method certainly looked the more solid of the two. Despite the gusts on the last day the canvas undulated happily, while Chris's rope roof looked ragged in comparison. But Chris's taller masts more than proved their worth: they ended up supporting nearly the entire roof – much more weight than they were designed to take. Chris's design as it was did not enable the *velum* to be furled when the wind got up. An unanswered question on the rope method is whether his design could be adapted to furl the canvas.

So whose was the most likely method to have been used? Rainer's method has more historical credibility. Its whole design and operation were understood and used by the sailors. Chris's rope method had no such historical backing. True, all the materials he used were available at the time and there is no evidence that the Romans did not do it this way. One of our other experts, historian Norma Goldman, is convinced that the Romans would have used the rope method. She cannot believe that, with their enterprising spirit and desire to achieve the unachievable, they would have been defeated in their attempt to span the entire auditorium. It was so clearly in their VIP's interest that they did so, and the only way to span the big space, from all our experience and calculations, was to use ropes and to forget booms.

Whichever method they used in other amphitheatres, and it could have been both, the scale of the Romans' achievement was extraordinary. Only recently have modern engineers and architects managed to achieve anything approaching the size of the lightweight roofs that the Romans erected over their amphitheatres. Nowadays only those of Olympic and World Cup stadia exceed a 30-metre span. Because of modern materials such as high-strength steel cables, man-made fibres and textiles, modern lightweight roofs are able to stay out permanently and deal with strong winds and hurricanes. They are considered state-of-the-art design work. Two thousand years ago the *vela* were too.

THE INCAS

ADRIANA VON HAGEN

O N the eve of the Spanish invasion in 1532, the Inca empire was the largest in the Americas. Fresh from their conquest of Mexico and spurred by rumours of a kingdom of gold, the conquistadors sailed south to Peru, where they found their El Dorado. Within a decade of their landfall, the riches of the Incas had become the jewel of the Spanish crown.

THE LAST ANDEAN EMPIRE

No other ancient realm embodied such a patchwork of peoples and places or straddled such imposing and rugged terrain. The Pacific coast is arid but boasts rich fishing grounds and lush river valleys watered by rivers originating in the snow-covered Andes to the east. These oases, and the valleys that climb the foothills, provided the Incas with cotton, chilli peppers and maize. High above these valleys lay the puna, or grasslands, home to one of the empire's primary sources of wealth: the enormous alpaca herds that supplied wool to weave the fine cloth so highly esteemed by Andean peoples. On its eastern frontier Inca territory included the hilly cloud forest, source of products such as honey, exotic woods, the feathers of colourful birds and coca leaf.

The spectacular Inca citadel of Machu Picchu
perched high above the Urubamba river.

Archaeology has revealed that the Incas were the last, and the largest, of a series of Andean cultures that ruled over a wide territory only to collapse within the space of a few centuries; the Incas themselves ruled for less than a century. They and their predecessors rose to power because they controlled a widely scattered kaleidoscope of peoples, languages and resources united by age-old Andean social institutions and strategies of land management. Building on the knowledge of their ancestors, the Incas turned the Andean region into a fertile and productive territory. They canalized rivers and constructed irrigation networks and terraces that greatly increased the amount of land under cultivation.

But how did a ragtag band of gold-greedy Spanish soldiers of fortune topple such a powerful and productive empire in only a few months? Tawantinsuyu, the Incas' own name for their empire, hints at its vulnerability. The word means 'four parts', and it was indeed a loose confederation of ethnic groups linked to Cuzco, the capital, through conquests, alliances and kinship ties, both imagined and real.

Because none of the Andean peoples developed writing, we are forced to depend on Spanish colonial documents for first-hand, yet biased, accounts of the final years of the Inca empire. These histories or chronicles, written by the priests and soldiers who accompanied the conquistadors, are supplemented by the reports, inspections and legal documents of the colonial administration. Many of these men wrote about their adventures in reports, letters and even bestsellers that swept Europe. Through their words we can feel the basic texture of the Inca world, and sense the awe and bewilderment that beset the Spaniards as they faced a society so alien to theirs.

The vision left to us by the Europeans passed through a seriously flawed lens through which we, in turn, are forced to view the Incas. The sixteenth-century European mind-set was poorly equipped to handle this spectacular civilization; indeed, neither society had the intellectual tools to understand the other. Most disturbingly of all, the Spaniards found in the Andes a land where time itself had a different meaning. The Inca sense of history was cyclical, rhythmic, repetitive and patterned, and proved impenetrable to European attempts to recount the past as a series of events. Today, a critical reading of these sixteenth-century texts coupled with careful archaeology provides a structural skeleton of Inca history, while observations of the life of contemporary peoples provide insights into the cultural processes that powered the development of Andean civilization.

Cuzco's nobility and the provincial élite, the chroniclers' principal informants, glorified their past and embroidered details of Inca exploits, clouding the early first-hand accounts and what is known of the Incas today. Despite the exaggerations and prejudices of the Spanish chroniclers, however, we often turn to these early accounts in search of descriptions of Inca engineering or the majesty of Inca Cuzco. Many of the Spanish eye witnesses genuinely lamented the destruction wrought by the European invaders. The ravages of epidemics, civil war, famine and social disruption led to a major decline in Andean populations, estimated to have ranged from 6 million to 13 million before the arrival of the Spaniards. 'The wars, cruelties, pillaging and tyranny of the Spaniards have been such that if these Indians had not been so accustomed to order and providence they would all have perished and been wiped out,' wrote Pedro de Cieza de León, a soldier who travelled through the remains of Tawantinsuyu only a decade after its fall.

THE HANDIWORK OF DEMONS?

One of the most imposing Inca accomplishments is the temple-fortress of Sacsawaman, perched above Cuzco. It was among these megalithic stones that we began our search for clues to the secrets of Andean technology. How could the Incas have built this monument without the wheel, without iron tools; using what was, in essence, Bronze Age technology? Few ancient Andean monuments have elicted as much commentary or inspired as many interpretations, both by the earliest Europeans to see it and by modern visitors regaled by the imaginative tales of tour guides. Centuries earlier, the young Garcilaso de la Vega, the son of an Inca princess and a Spanish soldier, played among Sacsawaman's walls. In his subsequent chronicle he called Sacsawaman the 'greatest and most splendid building erected to show the power and majesty of the Incas…the grandeur of which would be incredible to anyone who had seen it. And even those who have seen it

Looking down on the city of Cuzco from the temple-fortress of
Sacsawaman. INSET The grand fortress and its huge stone ramparts –
the incredible accomplishment of Inca builders.

and considered it with attention imagine, and even believe, that it was made by
enchantment, the handiwork of demons, rather than of men.'

To some observers, only demons could have moved the Cyclopean limestone blocks, many weighing almost a hundred tonnes, and all with the proverbial
perfect Inca fit, that form the foundations of Sacsawaman's three sets of zigzagging
ramparts. These huge stone blocks have inspired fantastic tales of builders from
outer space, plant acids that dissolve stone, and Inca emperors wielding parabolic
mirrors that could split rocks using solar energy. At Sacsawaman we were joined
by American archaeologist Helaine Silverman of the University of Illinois at
Urbana-Champaign. Perched at a breathtaking 3500 metres above sea level,
Sacsawaman is very different from her usual milieu, the arid coastal plains of
Nazca on Peru's south coast. 'There's no need to search for other-worldly forces
to discover who built Sacsawaman', Silverman says. Almost five hundred years
ago, Cieza noted how many Inca labourers toiled to build Sacsawaman: 'Four
thousand of them quarried and cut the stones; six thousand hauled them with
great cables of leather and hemp; the others dug the ditch and laid the foundations, while still others cut poles and beams for the timbers.' Father Bernabé
Cobo, a Jesuit writing in the seventeenth century, said that the Inca emperor
Pachakuti employed four master masons and thirty thousand labourers. Others
said that Sacsawaman was such a monumental undertaking that it took fifty years
to build, or that it was still under construction on the eve of the Spanish invasion.

Above the ramparts lie the remains of three towers, two rectangular and one
round, that overlooked Cuzco. To the Spaniards, the ramparts resembled those of a
fortress, which it is still often called by modern writers. Cieza, however, called it a
'house of the sun' that 'should house everything imaginable'. Indeed, some eye
witnesses, writes John Hyslop in *Inka Settlement Planning,* reported seeing dozens
of storehouses containing 'arms, clubs, lances, bows, arrows, axes, shields, heavy
jackets of quilted cotton, and other weapons of different types'. Sacsawaman
apparently served both a religious and a military function. Today a wide esplanade
between the ramparts and an outcrop called Suchuna is the setting for a modern
re-enactment of the Inca winter solstice festival that draws thousands of tourists
every year.

Part of the Suchuna has been carved into steps called the Throne of the Inca. On the other side, the outcrop has been worn smooth by local children sliding down its polished face. To the north is an area that contains aqueducts, cisterns, tunnels, terraces, patios, stairs and buildings as well as a large reservoir that once supplied water to Cuzco.

PACHAKUTI: MYTH OR REALITY?

The chroniclers say that it was the Inca emperor Pachakuti who built Sacsawaman. But who was he, when did he live, and how did he recruit the labour to build the monument? Because of the cyclical, non-historical sense in which the Incas regarded their past, assigning dates before the European invasion is very difficult. Archaeology has shown us that some time in the early fifteenth century the Incas were one of many ethnic groups scattered across the Cuzco valley until – and here we move into the realm of Inca mythical history – they vanquished a rival people in a key battle that transformed them into a nation with an imperial destiny. Inca tradition says that a single man, Pachakuti, was the agent of this transformation, guiding the Inca armies out of their home in the valley of Cuzco and south to victory over the alpaca-rich kingdoms along the shores of Lake Titicaca. Pachakuti, the Spaniards' informants said, was a gifted administrator who invented the structure of Inca government. His vision extended to the planning and construction of imperial Cuzco, Sacsawaman and the royal estates of Pisaq, Ollantaytambo and Machu Picchu in the Urubamba valley.

But the scope of these accomplishments is so grand, so ambitious and so complete that scholars like Silverman now question whether such a person ever existed. Perhaps Pachakuti – whose name, after all, means 'world change'– represents instead a mythical figure who condenses the genius of several talented leaders who propelled Inca expansion across southern Peru. By the second half of the fifteenth century, Pachakuti's son Topa Inca had led his armies from the coastal valleys of what is today Chile northwards across Peru, defeating the Chimu, the largest and most powerful coastal domain to contest Inca expansion. By the reign

The Inca empire was the largest in the New World and included Peru, Bolivia, northern Chile, north-western Argentina, Ecuador and southern Colombia. The Inca road network stretched 14 000 miles.

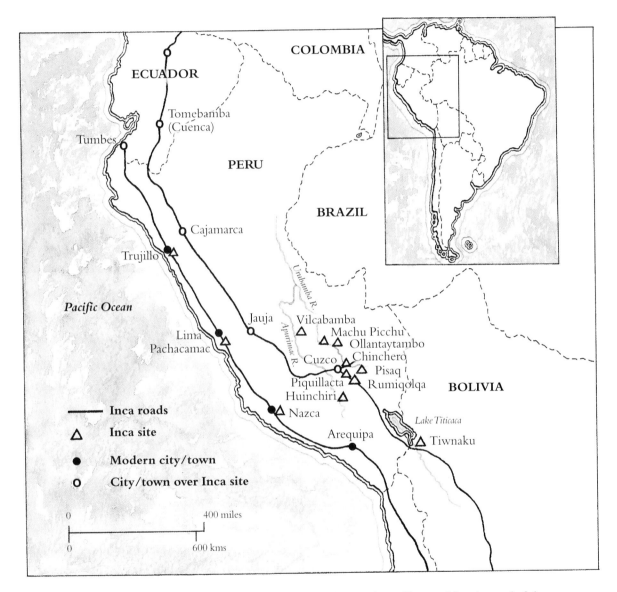

of Huayna Capac, who died around 1527, the realm of legend has been left behind. This emperor extended the empire even farther to include Bolivia and northern Ecuador. What is not in doubt is the speed of the Inca conquests after 1450. Their presence, marked by distinctive styles of architecture, pottery and weaving, is suddenly visible throughout much of the Andean region.

MILITARY AND ADMINISTRATIVE GENIUS

State policies towards conquered peoples were quite flexible, evolving in step with territorial expansion and reflecting the social, political and economic conditions of the regions and peoples which came under the umbrella of Tawantinsuyu. The Incas' foremost allies were those who had succumbed peacefully to Cuzco's imperial designs. Reprisals against peoples who defied them could be bloody, and were often followed by the forced resettlement of survivors hundreds of miles from their homelands and their replacement with loyal *mitmaqkuna*. This flexibility of Inca rule, coupled with Western attempts to fit this great and alien empire into a familiar scheme, explains why Inca rulers have been labelled everything from despotic monarchs to enlightened dictators. Tawantinsuyu has been called a feudal realm, a welfare state, an early experiment in socialism and a New World utopia.

The success of the Incas relied on more than just considerable military skill. They were adept at negotiation, and understood how to integrate new subjects into an effective and coherent whole that made life under the Incas structured and ordered. Their great gift lay in administering land, natural resources and, most importantly, people. In the vast labour pool of the conquered nations, the Incas found the soldiers to man their garrisons and armies; the masons and quarrymen to build and maintain their roads, bridges, towns, temples, irrigation canals and agricultural terraces; the colonists or *mitmaqkuna* to settle conquered areas, both providing labour and marking the Inca presence; the state officials to enforce Inca policies and to spread the language (Quechua) and their sun-worshipping religion; the bureaucrats to keep track of this human and natural wealth on *quipus,* accounting devices made of knotted string; and the men and women to weave the fine textiles that Inca officials would offer as gifts to cement alliances.

Foremost among the obligations of new citizens was to provide the Incas with a labour force through a tax called *mit'a,* on which the empire's productivity depended. Effective control of this vast and ever-growing army of workers lay at the heart of the Inca administrative genius. There was no doubt central direction, but the Incas managed to enfranchise and empower local groups by basing the

The huge limestone blocks of Sacsawaman's ramparts, many weighing
almost a hundred tonnes, were quarried, worked and moved without
the help of iron tools or the wheel.

institution of state labour on commonly shared Andean views of communal
work. This system was based on a sense of reciprocity that carefully balanced rights
and obligations, a way of bonding work partners in relationships called *ayni* that
persist in Andean communities to this day.

INCA QUARRYING

Beyond sheer numbers, how did these workers quarry and position the stones of
monuments such as Sacsawaman and achieve the famed fit? For over a decade
Swiss architect Jean-Pierre Protzen, who teaches at the University of California at
Berkeley, and Vincent Lee, an architect from Wyoming, have been exploring the
secrets of Inca stone working.

The great boulders that form Sacsawaman's zigzagging ramparts are of limestone, quarried from the many outcrops dotting the surrounding hills. Other

stones, such as the smaller andesite blocks that the Spaniards removed from Sacsawaman to build their churches and mansions in the city below, came from Rumiqolqa, a quarry 22 miles south-west of Cuzco. Protzen believes that the choice of rock type must have been important to the Inca masons because they quarried at sites that were difficult to reach and often quite distant from the work site. Inca regard for stone went beyond mere practical matters, Protzen notes, and it extended to a reverence that dictated choices of stone and styles of masonry for important walls or special structures. The Incas worshipped stone outcrops, boulders and particular upright stones. They regarded some stones as their ancestors and their myths are filled with accounts of brave warriors who were turned into stone. One legend tells of stones that grew tired, wept blood and refused to move. These are known as *piedras cansadas*, or weary stones, and there is one such stone near Sacsawaman – a massive limestone outcrop carved with steps and benches.

At Rumiqolqa Protzen found remains of Inca roads and ramps leading to the quarry area, but traces of ancient quarrying have been largely obliterated because the site is still worked today. Protzen thinks the Inca quarrymen followed natural fractures to extract the stone and may have used bronze crowbars to break out stones, or wooden sticks, like modern quarrymen. The quarries are littered with stones in different stages of production. The Incas shipped their finished stones to construction sites in Cuzco, where they are found in the finely wrought walls of Loreto Street and at the Qorikancha, the city's holiest shrine.

OLLANTAYTAMBO: A ROYAL ESTATE

Another, even more impressive, source of Inca building stone was the rock falls of Kachiqata. Blocks from this quarry were used to build Pachakuti's estate at Ollantaytambo, 3 miles upstream from Kachiqata on the opposite bank of the Urubamba river. The chroniclers tell us that in the Urubamba valley north of Cuzco the Inca kings founded their royal estates and embarked on their most elaborate land reclamation projects, traces of which still sculpt the valley today. In Pisaq, for instance, agricultural terraces sweep down the hillsides below the ruins

OVERLEAF The Urubamba valley, a source of Inca building stones and the town of Ollantaytambo. INSET A large monolith abandoned en route to the building site.

and the remains of retaining walls can be seen along the river banks downstream from the modern town, where the Urubamba still runs straight. 'This valley excels all others in Peru,' wrote Garcilaso, 'so that all the Inca kings ... made it their garden and haunt of pleasure and recreation ....'

The Patakancha river divides Ollantaytambo into the temple hill to the west and the town to the east; the latter is the only Inca settlement whose dwellings are still occupied today. Rising high above the town, the temple hill housed a religious precinct surrounded by a wall, probably to restrict access rather than to defend the site. The approach to Ollantaytambo from the east is fortified, however; these elaborate defences were probably built in 1537 during the Inca uprising against the Spanish invaders, when Ollantaytambo became the *de facto* capital of the rebels. After a long siege, the troops, commanded by Manco Inca, another of Huayna Capac's sons, repaired to the lower Urubamba valley where they established Vilcabamba as the capital of the ill-fated neo-Inca state.

The Spanish siege of Ollantaytambo apparently cut short an ambitious remodelling plan. On the temple hill the sector surrounding the Wall of the Six Monoliths, probably the foundations of a sun temple, is strewn with massive blocks of andesite and rhyolite that range from raw and partially worked stones to finished blocks which the Inca architects had removed from earlier constructions. Behind the Wall of the Six Monoliths lies the staging area for a 350-metre-long ramp that drops 50 metres to the valley floor, buttressed by a retaining wall 16 metres high at its tallest point. Ollantaytambo's builders used this ramp to drag stones up to the construction site from the rock falls of Kachiqata.

Unlike Rumiqolqa, Kachiqata is not a quarry in the true sense. Rather, Inca quarrymen picked blocks from rock falls, preshaped them and dispatched them to Ollantaytambo. Protzen spent several weeks camped in the quarries of Kachiqata, studying how Inca quarrymen and stonemasons worked these rockfalls. During his wanderings, he discovered one rose rhyolite block anchored in place by a 10-metre-high retaining wall. It is scored with work marks shaped like shallow depressions or pans. In an experiment, it took Protzen just under two hours of pounding with a hammerstone to shape a pan 15 centimetres square and 25 millimetres deep; he estimates that Inca quarrymen spent two to three weeks

preshaping Kachiqata's largest blocks. At this rate, he assesses it would have taken some eight months for fifteen crews of twenty workers each to rough out 150 blocks of rose rhyolite. There must have been hundreds of men working at Kachiqata at any given moment, the sound of hammerstones on rock echoing through the valley. But others have their own theories.

Ivan Watkins, who teaches geoscience at St Cloud State University in Minnesota, believes that the Incas could not have used hammerstones to cut and shape stones. He claims that they used solar energy focused with large parabolic mirrors. To test his ideas we set up Watkins' two silver mirrors on an Ollantaytambo street. Wearing protective goggles and asbestos gloves he tried to split a stone, but only succeeded in scorching a piece of wood. Watkins told us that the secrets of parabolic mirror technology had died with the last Inca emperor, who apparently had nothing better to do than personally cut and shape the thousands of stones quarried for the monuments of Tawantinsuyu. Watkins ignores the rich descriptions left to us by Spanish eye witnesses. No doubt the Spaniards would have found such a technology miraculous and described it in their chronicles; indeed, this solar energy would have been a powerful weapon against the Spanish troops. Yet nowhere in the chronicles do we find accounts of armour-clad Spaniards scorched in their saddles by the rays of parabolic mirrors! Nor is there any archaeological evidence for such mirrors.

Suddenly, perhaps during the Spanish siege, the quarrymen, masons and rock-dragging crews stopped work at Kachiqata and abandoned some forty blocks in different stages of transport. Frozen in time, the blocks lie scattered along the ramps leading from the rock falls to a chute overlooking the Urubamba, in cornfields on either side of the river, and along the ramp leading up to the temple hill. Like the elaborately carved outcrop at Sacsawaman, these abandoned blocks are called 'weary stones' by the modern inhabitants of Ollantaytambo, who hold them sacred.

Kachiqata's highest rock fall rises 900 metres above the valley floor. The entire area is criss-crossed by the remains of an elaborate 5-mile-long network of ramps and roads along which the quarrymen dragged the stones – some weighing close to 100 tonnes – from the rock falls to a chute or slide overlooking the

Urubamba. Here, one block is still wedged in the steep chute, which drops 250 metres to the valley floor.

For many years, Protzen has speculated that the Incas must have dragged the stones along a prepared roadway between the river crossing site and the temple hill. Indeed, some of the stones scattered in the fields are aligned with the temple hill ramp. Even more revealingly, on the temple hill he found stones that showed evidence of dragging. To resolve this issue, we sponsored an excavation by archaeologists from the Cuzco office of Peru's National Institute of Culture on the site of one of the abandoned blocks lying halfway between the river and the temple hill ramp. These excavations showed that this 3-metre-long block, which Protzen estimates weighs around 9 tonnes, was being moved lengthwise over a bed of loose rocks on top of a hard, prepared roadbed of packed gravel and earth. Masons had cut the block's bottom face to a smooth, slightly convex shape that showed clear drag marks, indicating that it was moving away from the quarry and towards the temple hill. Not only did we now have the first evidence for a prepared roadway, but the excavations did not reveal any evidence of wooden sleds, rollers or rails. Nor did the exposed surfaces of the block show any notches, grooves or bosses for the attachment of ropes. These are often found on stones at Ollantaytambo and Sacsawaman, and Protzen suggests that they were used to attach ropes to move the rocks into place at the construction site rather than to ship them from the quarry.

MOVING STONES AT OLLANTAYTAMBO

The next questions we set out to tackle were: how did the Incas organize the labour to drag these huge stones once they had reached the construction site? How did they attach the ropes to the stones? And how many people did it take to haul blocks that often weighed more than 100 tonnes? Helping Protzen in his investigations was Edward Franquemont, an anthropologist who has spent several years living in the community of Chinchero near Cuzco. These questions, says Franquemont, have produced intense debate among archaeologists and even among the chroniclers: 'And the question of how [the stones] were conveyed to the site is no less difficult a problem, since they had no oxen and could not make wagons; nor would oxen and wagons have sufficed to carry them', wrote the Jesuit chronicler Cobo. Some scholars have suggested that the Incas used log rollers, but the principle of the wheel, linked to rollers, was never used by the Incas. Furthermore, rollers would seem to be of dubious value on the steep ramps, roads and chutes that confronted the Incas on the journey between Kachiqata and Ollantaytambo. The real answer is probably much simpler: the Incas used their highly organized work crews to drag the stones, using ropes. The Spaniards saw similar large stones moved by native labourers during the construction of Cuzco's cathedral, using, according to Gutierrez de Santa Clara, 'much human labour and great ropes of vine and hemp', some, adds Diego de Trujillo, as 'thick as a leg'. Like so much of Inca technology, transporting stone was based on well-honed human skills, strength and organization, not on any special tools.

Protzen estimates that it required a force of 1780 people to drag the largest Kachiqata block, which weighs approximately a hundred tonnes, up the ramp to the temple hill. But the question that stumped both him and the film crew is what happened to these block draggers, a human train stretched almost 180 metres along the ramp, once they reached the top of it? Protzen speculates that if the coefficient of friction was reduced it would have been possible to decrease the pulling crew and move the stone from behind, with levers, to form a smaller work crew. At the same time, the Incas may have installed wooden turning posts at the top of the ramp. The ropes would have turned around these posts and the labour force could then have been redirected down the ramp.

How did the Incas organize the labour? The communities that nowadays occupy the former Inca heartland still order their lives on similar principles, which presented us with an ideal opportunity. We challenged members of these communities with three major tasks and left them to devise their own solutions. First we wanted to move stones along the ramps below the quarry and down the dramatic chute or slide to the river's edge; second, we asked them to move a stone across the river; and third, we needed to understand what would be involved in moving a very large stone.

Since we didn't want to disturb any stones already shaped by the Incas and abandoned along the ramp below the quarry, we moved only unworked natural boulders that we found on the hill near the ramp. Weighing about one tonne, none was large by Inca standards. Throughout our rock-moving experiments in Ollantaytambo we were assisted by David Canal, head of the local community. He assembled a group of some sixty-five men from Ollantaytambo and from Kachiqata, a small village below the quarry. As we were to discover, these numbers represented a great deal more labour than was actually necessary.

After beginning the day in true Inca fashion with a prayer and an offering to the Apus – the gods believed to reside on sacred mountain peaks – and several rounds of strong drink, the crews worked quickly in a democratically organized group that seemed to have no leader other than a master rigger who supervised the tying of the ropes. Most of the work on the ramp was accomplished very simply, with lots of laughter and shouting, by wrapping the rope around the stone and dragging it across wooden rails or loose, fist-sized stones thrown down to act as bearings. Occasionally, the work crew tumbled the stones rather than dragging them. As each stone reached the top of the steep chute, the men untied the rope and used it as a sling to launch the stone into the mouth of the chute. In this fashion, we launched three stones. They gained momentum rapidly as they bounced down the chute and shattered into several pieces at the bottom, damaging one farmer's cornfield. No doubt our stones were much more fragile than the hard Kachiqata rhyolite that the Incas used; none the less, this was almost certainly not the way the Incas lowered their carefully chosen and preshaped stones to the river's edge! Under more expert guidance, the Incas probably moved the stones carefully down the chute, with work crews stationed at intervals to nudge them along.

Our next challenge was to move a much larger and undeniably Inca stone. After receiving permission from the National Institute of Culture, we selected one from the town of Ollantaytambo. This massive, highly polished and finished stone weighed about 15 tonnes and had been moved several decades ago to its present location, about 30 centimetres below the surface of the cobbled street. First, Canal had dug a small trench around the stone; then, on the appointed day, he assembled a crew of nearly 350 men, women and children. Many of the men wore the distinctive black knee breeches, short red jackets and knitted caps of neighbouring villages, while some of the women carried babies slung from brightly coloured shawls on their backs. A festive atmosphere developed spontaneously at the work-site, with curious tourists looking on and local people offering advice to the work crew. By mid-morning, the master rigger had wrapped ropes several times around the stone and set up six long pull lines for the work crew to haul.

As Canal sounded the baleful tone of a *pututu* conch shell trumpet to signal the start of each tugging session, another dozen or so workers wielding wooden levers tried to force the reluctant stone out of its hole. For over an hour the crews swayed and rocked as they tugged and tried to prise the stone loose, but all to no avail. We began to think we had stumbled on our first failure in re-creating Inca labour. Finally, however, the stone wiggled and shifted two centimetres and we discovered what had been holding the rock firmly in place: a boss, one of the protrusions that Inca stonemasons shaped on stones to help move them into position at the work site. With a great cheer the crew finally heaved the stone out of its hole and, running, dragged it down the cobbled streets, leaving John Hazard, our cameraman, in a cloud of dust. Did the people of Ollantaytambo ever doubt their ability to free the Inca block ? Canal was surprised by the idea. 'No, of course not,' he said. 'People like us put it there, so people like us can make it move.'

This experiment had ably demonstrated one of the true legacies of the Inca empire. Throughout the Andes, large groups of men and women still assemble to perform the community labour tax which they levy upon themselves, combining work and festivities for the common good. In Inca times, labour for the state was socially based rather than an individual burden. 'The Incas arranged and established this work so that the people came to consider it recreational and enjoyable,' wrote Cobo. 'And this is one of the things in which the Incas provided their genius: they were able to set up an occupation requiring so much work and effort in such a way that it came to be considered an enjoyable and pleasurable practice.' Today, teams of workers plant communal fields, construct community buildings, and repair roads; in one case, perhaps unique in the whole world, the community of Huinchiri continues to maintain the swaying suspension bridge across the Apurimac river that was entrusted to its care over half a millennium ago.

A BRIDGE TO BRING PEOPLE TOGETHER

Our search for the secrets of Inca engineering now led us away from the major monuments of Inca civilization to this remote community of scattered farmsteads, six hours south-west of Cuzco over bone-rattling roads. For nearly five hundred years the people of Huinchiri have annually assembled materials and gathered themselves into large labour crews to renew this extraordinary rope bridge, even though a modern steel bridge lies only a few hundred metres upstream. Here we did not just use our powers of Western reasoning to re-create a lost technology from evidence scratched into stone; instead, we witnessed a technology that is still vital and functioning, where indigenous know-how is still a part of life, untainted by European principles. As we saw Huinchiri mobilize materials and human resources in ways we would never have imagined, we realized that we were very close to the heart of the genius of Andean technology. And after we had admired the newly completed bridge, we also understood that, for the surrounding communities, the bridge was more about bringing people together than about crossing a river.

WEAVERS OF ROPES

Although the bridge building usually takes place during the rainy season, the entire procedure was carried out for us in three very full days of August 1994. Despite the fact that the old structure that dangled across the chasm was in very sorry shape, and obviously in urgent need of replacement, we were concerned that this shift in date might affect the availability of resources, or, even worse, that it might erase the connection of the bridge to its rightful place in the annual ritual calendar that is so important to these communities. In fact, though, the materials proved easier to acquire than usual. And while no doubt something was lost in divorcing the work from its place in the ritual calendar, the anthropologists had more trouble with this than the people of Huinchiri did.

On each of the three days a different principle of labour organization was used to accomplish distinctly different goals. The first day mobilized masses of people from four different communities to make cables; the second focused on the specialization of a single village to stretch these cables across the gorge; and the third depended on a single individual with an inherited specialization to weave the structure of the bridge. These three principles are well known in the Andes, yet it is rare for a single task to encompass all three.

Construction actually began before we arrived. Each household set to work making their share of rope, called *k'eswa*, from the dry flower stalks of the *q'oya* grass, which gives the bridge its name: K'eswachaca, or bridge of rope. Women spin-ply the stalks between the palms of their hands to produce a two-ply rope about as thick as a finger and 50 metres long.

On the first day, the communities of Quehue and Choquehue assembled with their ropes on the west bank of the river, while Huinchiri and Chaupibanda met on the east. There were nearly five hundred people, all working in friendly competition; the work site, spread along the road on either side of the gorge, felt more like a carnival. People stood around in small groups, renewing friendships and beginning flirtations, while fruit-sellers plied their trade and chased away stray dogs. Groups of men from each community stretched the ropes out along the road in three groups of twenty-four, and then twisted the strands tightly into cables that were subsequently braided together. The finished rope-braids were about 20 centimetres in diameter; it took eight strong men to carry each one down to the bridge site.

As each household handed over its quota of rope, one man noted their contribution in a book. Watching him, Franquemont said that this man's job was like that of the Inca *quipucamayoc*, or *quipu* master, whose task it was to tally the Inca goods kept in storehouses throughout the realm and account for Tawantinsuyu's labour force. The goods, symbols of Inca wealth and largesse, were used to clothe, arm and sustain passing armies and to feed workers engaged in state enterprises.

The first task – making the ropes: a woman spins a
two-ply rope between her hands while the men lay the thicker ropes
along the road in order to twist them into thick cables.

Neither the Incas nor their ancestors developed writing. Instead they used *quipus,* perhaps one of the most remarkable artifacts of the pre-industrial world. As an object, the *quipu* is unimposing: a series of coloured yarns tied together, covered with clusters of knots and attached to a larger central cord. But we know from the Spaniards who watched the *quipucamayocs* that these cords and knots trapped Inca thought in a pure, highly abstracted form. 'By these recording devices and registers they conserved the memory of their acts,' wrote Cobo, 'and the Inca's overseers and accountants used them to remember what had been received and consumed. A bunch of these *quipos* served them as a ledger or note-book.' Edward Franquemont explains that a decimal numerical system was coded on to the strings of many *quipus.*

However, *quipus* were much more complex than that. For instance, Cieza noted that elders used them 'to make and arrange songs so that thereby it might be known in the future what had taken place in the past'. In fact, much of the Inca 'history' passed on to the Spanish chroniclers probably represents such coded information retrieved many decades later. A further, as yet undeciphered, system allowed the recording of grammar and syntax, context and content, and the cause, effect and motivation underlying Inca events. In many ways, then, the Incas were the world's first information-dependent society. But after the invasion, the rich code of the *quipu* became a simple mnemonic notepad and the Inca software developers reduced to mere bean counters.

SPANNING THE GORGE

As work continued on the bridge, our crew and entourage of assistants helped rig a steel cable adjacent to the bridge so that our cameraman could film the bridge builders at eye level. Supervising this operation was another of our consultants, Frenchman Philippe Petit, highwire walker and master rigger. Using sign language and bits of *k'eswa* rope as props, Petit explained his craft to Donato Tapia, head of the community of Huinchiri, while Tapia described to Petit how the villagers would build the bridge at Huinchiri.

In Inca times, this was a minor, out-of-the-way river crossing on the upper reaches of the Apurimac, small compared to the great Inca suspension bridges that awed and terrified the Spanish invaders. The most elegant solution that Europe could devise at this time to the considerable engineering challenges posed by a large bridge was the arch, a heavy stone structure that pushed out against massive abutments and carried travellers up and over the span. While long, graceful, multi-arch spans show considerable ingenuity, the principle of the suspension bridge must then have seemed an impossibility. Yet Inca suspension bridges spanned gaps as wide as 45 metres with a delicate, web-like structure. The stout main cables were made of basketry reeds tied together into a floor and lashed to handrail cables with small ropes. The entire structure pulled at its abutments with its load, and sagged towards the middle.

Worse yet, these bridges swayed in the strong winds that rushed down Andean canyons, and they bounced up and down and side to side with the steps of travellers. Several of the great Inca suspension bridges were maintained into the nineteenth century, to inspire visitors with the sheer audacity of an attempt to span a rushing river on strands of grass held in place by clever knots. Sadly there are no accounts of how these more recent bridges were built and maintained. Original construction of one of these great bridges must have been an enormous undertaking: in 1534 the Spaniards watched Inca troops spend twenty days rebuilding a bridge under the direction of a *chacacamayoc*, or bridge master. After completion, each bridge was staffed by attendants who helped people cross, and a local community was entrusted with its care.

Huinchiri was one such community and the second day of our celebration belonged exclusively to it, although the hillsides were filled with onlookers from various neighbouring villages. The men of Huinchiri specialize in stretching the cables tightly across the canyon. Surprisingly, they didn't use the old bridge as the lead rope to pass the new cables across, but rather cut it down into the rushing river before starting with the new cables. The braided cables went across the canyon tied to a lead rope and were anchored to the beams behind the abutments on the east side. Then the men divided into two crews that each took charge of two of the four braids on the west side. Next, amid much heaving and shouting, both sides pulled the ropes, wrapping the slack around the stone beams on either side. This went on for nearly the entire day until the base of the bridge had been established: four heavy braids made of grass stretched tightly across the chasm. Before the end of the day the men had also stretched two hand grip cables across the chasm.

Throughout, there was one unwavering presence: the *misayoc,* or ritual specialist, charged with keeping the project upright in the spiritual realm. The *misayoc* tended a ritual *mesa* – a cloth spread out on the ground – from which he consulted and indulged the spiritual forces with a series of offerings called *pagasqas,* or payments. Some were simply beer or *trago* (cane alcohol), the universal lubricant for all Andean activities, while others involved offerings of maize, cotton, coca leaves and animal fetuses. Because Franquemont was our only Quechua speaker he was asked to put together several of these bundles of *pagasqas* under the *misayoc*'s supervision. One of the main elements of a good *pagasqa* is plenty of alcohol, not a drop of which ever makes it into the bundles. By noon the *misayoc* and his attendants were all quite drunk, which is precisely the altered state they were trying to achieve. The *misayoc*'s power over the work flow sometimes frustrated the film crew, who would just get set up for a difficult shot only to find that work had stopped, while at other times the *misayoc*'s commands to go ahead seemed to override the need to set up equipment or change positions.

On the final day, one very special *pagasqa* involved the sacrifice of a sheep to the powerful mountain gods, or Apus, that held sway over the bridge and its people. After a lengthy bout of drinking, the *chacacamayoc,* who had learnt the skill from his father, headed for the bridge. He straddled all four braided cables at the mouth of the bridge, reached out as far as he could and lashed a wooden spreader across the bottom of the braids to establish spacing, then lashed them together. He worked his way across the bridge while a second man followed, lashing the handrail cable to the floor with a simple stitch. By the time they were a third of the way across a second team of floor lashers had begun from the opposite bank. After the two teams had met and finished the lashing they laid a floor of mats over the base, and the newly re-created bridge was complete. The bridge masters were the first across, followed by village dignitaries.

Spanning the gorge: the first six ropes stretched across;
lashing the handrails; and the final test – crossing the newly
completed bridge.

We debated who would be the first *gringo* across the bridge; Petit, the tightrope walker, seemed a natural choice. But the bridge builders came trotting back across to our side and nominated our associate producer, Julia Cort, as 'god-mother' of the bridge, with the honour of being the first across. She had sworn not to set foot on the bridge, but was somehow swept across by the cheering crowd, and we followed. The words of Pedro Sancho, Francisco Pizarro's secretary and one of the first Europeans to describe such a bridge, came back to haunt us as we gingerly made our way across the swaying bridge: 'The crossing appears dangerous because the bridge sags with its long span…and when the bridge is being crossed it trembles very much; all of which goes to the head of someone unaccustomed to it.'

ANDEAN RELIGION, INCA GOLD

Today most Andean communities depend for their rituals on *trago*, a powerful cane alcohol that is much cheaper than the beer produced in Cuzco. In the past, *chicha*, or fermented maize beer, was indispensable for religious ceremonies. Indeed, maize was one of the most important ritual crops of the Andes, and the Incas devoted many of their agricultural terraces to this plant. At any given ritual the Incas consumed enormous quantities of *chicha*.

In modern Huinchiri, as well as in other Andean communities, people practise the Christianity imposed by the Spaniards but also worship the spirits residing in hills, crags, caves, springs, rivers and lakes linked to the forces of nature. Offerings to these spirits are made before embarking on any journey or under-taking, much as we saw at Huinchiri. People offer *pagasqas* to Pachamama, or mother earth, and to the Apus, the most powerful deities of all, who from their mountaintop sanctuaries are perceived to control weather and thus the fertility of crops and herds.

The Inca state religion was a solar cult, often imposed alongside the shrines or *wacas* of conquered peoples. In their strategy of conquest the Incas incor-porated local deities into their pantheon and took the idols of subject peoples to

Cuzco, where they were kept as honoured hostages and paraded around the city's plazas during festivities. The Qorikancha, or Golden Enclosure, was Cuzco's sun temple and holiest shrine. No other structure in Inca Cuzco incited Spanish gold fever like the riches plundered in 1533 from this temple. By the time Cieza reached Cuzco the Qorikancha had been stripped of its treasures, but those who had seen it before its ransacking told him that it was 'one of the richest temples in the whole world…there was an image of the sun, of great size, made of gold, beautifully wrought and set with many precious stones.' Below the temple 'was a garden in which the earth was lumps of fine gold, and it was cunningly planted with stalks of corn that were made of gold…there were many tubs of gold and silver and emeralds, and goblets, pots, and every kind of vessel all of fine gold….' Here the Incas worshipped the image of the sun as well as other celestial deities such as the moon, the Pleiades and the rainbow. The temple's finest construction is a curved wall built of blocks of shimmering dark grey andesite. 'In all Spain I have seen nothing that can compare with these walls and the laying of these stones,' wrote Cieza.

CUZCO: CENTRE OF THE REALM

Not all of Cuzco's buildings were as elaborate as the Qorikancha. Sancho, one of the first Spaniards to enter the city in 1533, noted:

> *Most of the buildings are built of stone and the rest have half their façade of stone. There are also many adobe houses, very efficiently made, which are arranged along straight streets on a cruciform plan. The streets are all paved, and a stone-lined water channel runs down the middle of each street. Their only fault is to be narrow; only one mounted man can ride on either side of the channel.*

Cuzco was the ritual centre and architectural showcase of the Inca empire. Around the city's Huaycaypata, or dual central plaza, lay the fine stone palaces of the rulers, as well as public buildings, temples and shrines. This ceremonial core

The Spanish church of Santo Domingo lies over the remains of
Qorikancha, Cuzco's holiest shrine. It was stripped of its treasures by
the Spanish invaders in 1533.

was populated by members of the nobility, assembled in ten descent groups
known as *panacas*. According to chroniclers, each *panaca* included the descendants
of an Inca king. His successor formed his own *panaca*. Population estimates for
greater Cuzco range from forty thousand to a hundred thousand. Most people,
however, lived outside in scattered hamlets set among cultivated fields and
terraces, storehouses and irrigation canals.

By Huayna Capac's reign the *panacas* had grown extremely powerful. The
chroniclers say that they built palaces in Cuzco and lived off the produce from
royal estates. On a ruler's death, his *panaca* tended to his mummified remains. All of
this fascinated Cobo: 'The riches that were collected and gathered together just in
the city of Cuzco…were incredible…especially since each king tried to surpass
all of his ancestors in having a richer, more illustrious and splendid house than
they did.'

Ancestor worship in the Andes is several thousand years old, explains Peruvian bio-archaeologist Sonia Guillen. The Incas preserved the remains of the deceased in a form that closely resembled the person in life. The mummification process, says Guillen, included evisceration and the filling of the body cavities with cotton or plant fibre, which not only conserved the shape of the body but also helped prevent further deterioration. The skin was treated with salts or some sort of unguent, or the bodies may have been smoked. This entire process was probably a lengthy one, says Guillen, and the mummies required constant upkeep. Periodically, the mummies were wrapped in new clothing, presented with offerings of food and drink and taken on ritual excursions to shrines around Cuzco maintained by their descendants.

Among these shrines is Qqenqo, a limestone outcrop riddled with caves, niches and carvings. A small semi-circular plaza with the remains of nineteen niches lies on one side of the outcrop and faces a sacred, upright rock surrounded by a platform wall. A cave inside the outcrop is reached by tunnels and has an altar-like carving. The mummies of the ancestor-kings may have been seated in these niches, where rites were carried out in their honour, offerings proffered and libations – blood or *chicha* – poured down the zigzagging channels carved into the upper part of Qqenqo.

MACHU PICCHU

To ensure that the ancestor's mummies would be properly cared for the *panacas* had luxurious estates, among them Machu Picchu. When the American explorer Hiram Bingham stumbled upon it in 1911 its remote setting high above the Urubamba river led him to believe that he had found the lost capital of the Incas. But sixteenth-century Spanish colonial land tenure documents suggest that it may have been a royal estate of Pachakuti.

Machu Picchu, Silverman and Franquemont tell us, is not in fact an isolated site; it lies on a daring road linking a series of citadels strung along the peaks of the high jungle. Among fountains, carved stones and finely fitted walls, Machu Picchu's landscape architects harmonized architecture and sacred geography. The trapezoid – hallmark of Inca architecture – is found in the site's doorways and windows, many of which look onto distant peaks and the Urubamba river below. Although elaborate Inca stonework may seem ubiquitous to most visitors, this masonry style was reserved for the most important buildings in and around Cuzco, the Urubamba valley and a handful of provincial capitals. Most Inca constructions, in fact, are of fieldstones set in mud mortar, while on the coast they built in adobe. Nevertheless, in the span of a century, the Inca stamped their distinctive architecture on the Andes. 'One should think that a single architect has built this large number of monuments,' wrote the nineteenth-century German naturalist Alexander von Humboldt.

Although we shall never be certain what Machu Picchu's function was, its many carved rocks, chain of sixteen spring-fed fountains and spectacular setting indicate that it was more than a simple Inca outpost on the fringes of the empire's eastern domains. Its inaccessible location a mile above the torrential Urubamba river, defensive walls, guarded entrance gates, bridge and dry moat probably served to limit access to what was a highly religious site rather than to deter would-be invaders. Curiously, the Spaniards never reached Machu Picchu. When the conquistadors set off in pursuit of the rebel Incas ensconced in the jungle fastness of Vilcabamba they took the Inca road leading north-west from Ollantaytambo down to the Lucumayo river, following the Urubamba downstream from Machu Picchu to Vilcabamba. The conquistadors never travelled the route high above the left bank of the Urubamba, used today by trekkers hiking to Machu Picchu.

THE INCA ROAD SYSTEM

Some of the most remarkable stretches of Inca road ever constructed connected Machu Picchu to Cuzco. But this road was only a small part of the 14000-mile-long network that formed the nervous system of the Inca empire. Two major roads, one highland and one coastal, carried goods, people and information from the ends of the realm to Cuzco; smaller, lateral roads connected the main roads at several points. The sophistication of this communication system, which rivalled that of Rome, was noted by the Spaniards who travelled it during the early years of the invasion: 'Oh, can anything comparable be said of Alexander, or of any of the mighty kings who ruled the world, that they built such a road,' marvelled Cieza. It ran

> through deep valleys and over mountains, through piles of snow, quagmires, living rock, along turbulent rivers; in some places it ran smooth and paved, carefully laid out; in others over sierras, cut through the rock, with walls skirting the rivers, and steps and rests through the snow; everywhere it was clean swept and kept free of rubbish, with lodgings, storehouses, temples to the sun, and posts along the way.

The system connected some of the most formidable terrain in the world. In places it required massive stone embankments plastered against the sides of steep rock faces, like the bridge at Machu Picchu or the road leading from Machu Picchu to the Temple of the Moon below Huayna Picchu. Elsewhere the Incas carved tunnels through living rock or built causeways across marshy areas. Great caravans of llamas travelled these roads. *Chasquis,* or messengers running in relay, could cover 150 miles a day, delivering messages and even fresh fish to the emperor's table in Cuzco: 'neither swift horses nor mules could carry the news with more speed than these messengers on foot,' said Cieza.

ACHIEVING THE INCA FIT

This amazing road system is one of many ways in which the Incas used their engineering skills to master the challenges of the rugged Andean topography. But we still had not determined how they achieved the remarkable fit between stones. 'And if one went on to wonder,' mused Garcilaso, 'how such large stones could be fitted together so that the point of a knife could scarcely be inserted between them, there would be no end to our pondering.' Vince Lee has been pondering this problem for over a decade. Although Protzen has shown us convincingly that Inca masons shaped boulders with hammerstones, what is not clear is how the builders were able to lower these massive blocks into position, and fit them to neighbouring stones so accurately. After spending several months studying Sacsawaman's blocks, noting the sequences in which they were lowered into place and the curious indentations and bosses found at the bases of some of them, Lee developed a theory inspired by the way in which builders of traditional log cabins notch the trunks to each other using a sort of draughtsman's compass. This method is called scribing and coping. Lee postulates that the Inca compass, or scribe, was made of string, wood and a stone plumb bob. It would enable them to transfer the precut shape of an upper stone on to the stone already in place below it by moving the upper end of the stick along the precut surface of the upper stone. With the plumb bob centred in its hole, the lower end of the stick would precisely duplicate the profile of the upper stone.

Protzen, however, believes that the Incas used a trial-and-error method, much as the one described by the chronicler José de Acosta in 1589:

> *And what I admire most is that, although these [stones] in the wall I am talking about are not regular but very different among themselves in size and shape, they fit together with incredible precision without mortar. All this was done with much manpower and much endurance in the work, for to adjust one stone to another until they fit together, it was necessary to try the fit many times, the stones not being even or full.*

Central to Protzen's trial-and-error hypothesis is the phrase 'it was necessary to try the fit many times'; he believes that the masons shaped and reshaped, fitted and refitted the stones over and over again until they reached the desired fit. Unlike Lee's scribing and coping, Protzen argues that his method does not require the use of tools or implements of which no traces have been found.

To see how effective trial and error is, we challenged Protzen to restore a double-jambed doorway in the residential sector of Inca Ollantaytambo. Using hammerstones, he had demonstrated in an earlier experiment that it took twenty minutes to dress and finish an andesite block measuring 25 x 25 x 30 centimetres and another ninety minutes to dress the other three sides and to cut five edges. He

Vince Lee demonstrates to Helaine Silverman and Philippe Petit his theory of how the Incas achieved the tight fit of their stones. He made a string compass, or scribe, and used a stone bob on his plumb line.

fitted this block to another one, which he had pounded for ninety minutes to create a bedding joint. Could he replicate this at Ollantaytambo?

The original town grid is made up of four long streets crossed by seven shorter ones, forming blocks. Each block contains two *kanchas,* or walled compounds, composed of four buildings surrounding a central courtyard. Entry to the compounds was through impressive double-jambed doorways topped by lintels. These doorways, reserved for the most elaborate Inca structures, indicate that Ollantaytambo's Inca residents were members of the nobility. But only one of these doorways has survived intact. The post-Inca occupants of the town have removed the lintels and destroyed the doorways to accommodate the hefty girth of farm animals native to Europe.

Protzen's doorway fronts Pata Calle, the last street on the town's west side. It was in reasonably good shape, and some of the original stones lay inside the *kancha* or on a terrace below the street. Protzen and his team used andesite from a quarry near Pisaq to contrast with the andesite that the Incas had used for the original doorway. Bedevilled by time constraints, the modern masons used steel chisels, mallets and bouchards to shape the stones. With hammerstones, Protzen reckons, it would have taken one or two days to shape each stone and the same amount of time to fit each block into place. But the greatest challenge was lifting and lowering the stones into position without damaging them. Protzen's workers used crowbars and miner's bars to roll the stones up on poles and drop them into position. 'Most likely,' Protzen says, 'this was not how the Incas did it. They must have had a "soft" way of handling the blocks, being able to move them with great care, slowly and very smoothly.'

Lee agrees with Protzen that the Incas used the trial-and-error method to build doorways such as the one in Ollantaytambo. But he doesn't think they used this method to build Sacsawaman's ramparts or other megalithic structures. He thinks it would have been 'horrendously tedious and inefficient. It does not seem likely that a people as well organized, efficient and clever as the Incas would have used such a cumbersome method unless there were no alternatives.' Protzen agrees that his method is laborious for Cyclopean masonry, but accuses Lee of projecting 'contemporary views of efficiency and least effort on to past civilizations. Time and effort clearly did not have the same value for the Incas as it does for us,' he says. None the less, he acknowledges that 'there is plenty of room for alternative explanations'.

Many of the chroniclers' detailed accounts support Protzen's trial-and-error method, although he acknowledges that this method is not an entirely satisfactory answer to the huge masonry blocks of Ollantaytambo, Sacsawaman or Machu Picchu. Although Lee had experimented in Wyoming with polystyrene blocks, he hadn't tried scribing and coping with real stones. He chose a site down-river from Ollantaytambo, where he and his team of nine masons spent three weeks fitting together boulders. Because the Incas often incorporated bedrock into their masonry, Lee picked an outcrop (stone A) to which he planned to fit a loose boulder (stone B) weighing about one tonne. Both were of green andesite, which proved much harder than the limestone of Sacsawaman or the rhyolite of Kachiqata. Cutting it, Lee says, was 'horrendously difficult', and a frustrated team of masons began calling the stones 'mistake No. 1' and 'mistake No. 2'.

Before scribing could take place, Lee's masons had to preshape the stones. This took five men some six hundred hours, by far the most time-consuming part of the experiment. As a shortcut, they used decidedly non-Inca steel chisels. But these, Lee says, cut so slowly that he was unsure if they were any faster than Inca hammerstones. Once the masons had preshaped the stones, stone B had to be moved into position, with its cut face roughly parallel to and the length of the scribe away from the matching face of stone A. Scribing stone B to stone A, recalls Lee, 'was almost an anti-climax'. It took Lee's crew a day and a half to scribe the stones, abandoning their steel hammers and chisels for tangerine-sized hammerstones to avoid unwanted chipping. When the scribing was finished, they moved stone B against stone A. 'The proverbial knife blade couldn't be inserted between the stones.'

Next, the crew preshaped stone C, which they planned to drop into an L-shaped seat cut into the top of stone A. L-shaped joints, explains Lee, must be scribed vertically, with the upper stone suspended above its intended seat. 'Most scepticism regarding the scribing method centres on this point,' he concedes. They slid stone C on to a scaffold of poles resting on wooden posts with forked tops, inserted shoring posts into the pockets and braced the stone securely before removing the scaffold. Again, scribing was the easiest part of the whole operation.

Although Lee admits that he and his team made lots of mistakes, 'we proved that scribing and coping works'. None the less, Lee admits that 'there is no way to know whether or not the Incas used the scribing and coping method, but I now believe they did — or something very much like it. The only alternatives to scribing are trial-and-error and templating [using a model to copy something accurately]. I have long thought trial and error impracticably laborious, applied to very large stones. Based on our experience here in Ollantaytambo, I now think it impossible.' Adds Protzen, 'Of all the alternatives I've heard, Lee's is the most convincing to date. He has demonstrated that it can work.'

Jean-Pierre Protzen using a hammerstone to shape a stone block;
Vince Lee demonstrating the tight fit of his stonework; and Protzen's answer
to our challenge – the completed doorway at Ollantaytambo.

MOVING STONES ACROSS THE URUBAMBA

We still had one mystery to resolve in Ollantaytambo. How did the Incas move the Kachiqata stones across the Urubamba? We know by the number and distribution of abandoned blocks that there were several places where they forded the river, and there were probably several roadways that brought the stones across the valley floor to the ramp leading up to the temple hill. Such an array of stones suggests that no single crew took an individual stone all the way from quarry to construction site, but that different crews took responsibility for parts of the journey in the same way that different communities worked on opposite sides of the river in Huinchiri. Some have suggested that rafts of wooden logs ferried boulders across the river, but these would probably have sunk in the shallow, rock-strewn torrent at the crossing site. Nor did we think it was feasible that the Incas diverted the river to avoid having to move the stones through it. (The technology, however, was not beyond them, since they had canalized the same river elsewhere.) Again, the truth is probably the simplest concept: they dragged the stones across.

We attempted a river crossing using large field stones about the same size as those we had launched down the chute. After considerable debate, we chose to cross at the widest, shallowest part of the river and set up elaborate safety procedures, including downstream catch lines and an inflatable raft staffed by experienced river runners. Even in the dry season, this is a challenging stretch of water navigated only by intrepid rafters. But our rock dragging crew found the danger exhilarating, and took a very direct approach. The riggers tied a strong net around the stone and brought three pull lines across to the opposite bank. Over 150 men waded into the water, and on command pulled the stone directly across the river at a steady rate. As the stone emerged from beneath the waters and appeared on the opposite bank, the men let out a great cheer. Although we had originally arranged for only one crossing, the scene was so dramatic that the film crew asked them to cross the river again with another stone. The men readily agreed, with one provision: that they be allowed to continue pulling the stone up to the road about half a mile away. This, they explained, was 'for pride', so that for years to come they could point out the stones and tell the story of the river crossing.

The team of over 150 men starting to pull the stone across
the widest and shallowest part of the Urubamba river.

Later that day we celebrated the success of our rock-pulling experiments
with a bullfight. The entire town converged on Ollantaytambo's small bullring,
where Canal had arranged for the valley's bravest bullfighters to tussle with the
region's fiercest bulls. Had we been Incas we would have hosted a lavish banquet
of Andean delicacies: llama and guinea pig spiced with aji peppers and accompanied by potatoes of all varieties, washed down with copious amounts of *chicha*.
Today, however, the Spanish sport of bullfighting often replaces the banquets
of old.

WOVEN WEALTH

Nowhere was the conflict of values and cultures more apparent than in the
Spanish quest for gold. 'Their only concern was to collect the gold and silver to
make themselves all rich…without thinking that they were doing wrong and
were wrecking and destroying,' wrote one chronicler, Cristóbal de Molina. After
the Spaniards ambushed the Inca emperor Atawalpa's troops in Cajamarca and
captured him, gold and silver poured in from all over the land in a bid to free the
ruler. But instead of releasing Atawalpa, the Spaniards, under the command of

Francisco Pizarro, strangled him. After melting down the gold they had amassed in Cajamarca, the Spaniards began searching for mines: 'There is no kingdom in the world so rich in precious ores,' noted Cieza, 'for every day great lodes are discovered, both of gold and of silver…It amazed me that the whole city of Cuzco and its temples were not of solid gold.' The Spaniards' insatiable quest for precious metals baffled the Incas. But equally puzzling to the Spaniards was that, for the Incas, gold and silver came second to cloth as symbols of wealth and power.

Textiles had the same meaning for the Incas as gold and literature had for the Spaniards. The ingenuity, creativity and sheer cultural energy invested by Andean people in cloth far exceeded any reasonable human impulse to elaborate and decorate what they wore. By the time of the Incas, textiles had developed into an all-purpose medium that could embody, record and convey a wealth of information far broader than that contained in the fashions and costumes of the Europeans. Distinctive styles of dress served to signal ethnic identity and allowed the Inca to distinguish his subjects. And, as with virtually all that the Incas controlled, their genius for co-ordination and management raised cloth production to levels never seen before.

To guarantee this vast output, the Incas deployed thousands of weaving specialists throughout the realm. The state supported special classes of male and female weavers who made a cloth called *qompi*, so fine that it dazzled even the Spaniards accustomed to the fine tapestries of Renaissance Europe. Among the weavers of fine cloth were the *aqlla,* who lived in *aqllawasi,* or residences of 'chosen women' located in Cuzco and strategically throughout the realm. Because these *aqllawasi* reminded the Spaniards of convents they called the women 'virgins of the sun', although many of these women were in fact awarded in marriage to men who had honoured the state. At the same time, each village made its own version of cloth, called *awasqa.*

After the invasion, *qompi* production lingered briefly with Church support, but was soon lost. *Awasqa,* however, has survived in the villages of the Andes as a kind of ethnic code that embodies and teaches many of the fundamental concepts of Inca thought. One such village is Chinchero, where Nilda Callañaupa learned to spin and weave. We commissioned her to weave an Inca *unku,* a tunic in a red,

LEFT An example of fine Inca weaving worn by the nobility. Clothing signalled status and ethnic identity. RIGHT A silver figurine wrapped in finely woven cloth, found in a mountain-top sanctuary in the Andes.

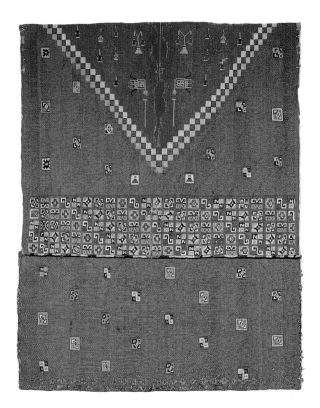

white and black checkerboard pattern that recalls the uniforms of Inca soldiers. Callañaupa wove the *unku* on an upright loom, the kind used by the Inca weavers of fine cloth. 'I may not be a virgin,' she told us, 'but I can weave *qompi*.'

AN EMPIRE IN DECLINE

The state devoted much of its cloth production to dressing its armies, reserving the finest, especially feather cloth, for them. Cloth played an important role in all aspects of warfare. Inca troops protected their bodies with quilted cotton and wore quilted cotton or wooden helmets. They fought with slings made of llama or alpaca fibre or *cabuya,* and carried shields of woven palm slats and cotton, sheathed with deerskin and decorated with fine cotton, wool or feather cloth.

The battles, like the costumes of the troops, were imbued with symbolism and ritual. The Spaniards took advantage of such rigid procedures, noting that the Inca forces launched their attacks during the full moon and paused at the new moon to honour the lunar deity. This highly structured and ritualized form of warfare was no match for the ambush tactics of the conquistadors. When Inca foot soldiers clashed for the first time with Spanish troops in Cajamarca, their quilted cotton armour could not thwart the lances and swords of Toledo steel wielded by Spaniards mounted on horses – creatures which they had never seen before.

There were other reasons, apart from superior weapons, that enabled the invaders to overthrow the lords of Cuzco in only a few months. Tawantinsuyu's fragile design, exacerbated by the speed of the Inca conquests and the empire's great size, made the empire unwieldy and impractical to govern centrally from Cuzco; this is probably why Huayna Capac decided to build a second capital in Tomebamba, today Ecuador. Even more serious, maintaining the royal estates of Cuzco's powerful *panacas* commanded considerable energy, detracting from more serious matters of state. Furthermore, the lack of rules governing succession to the throne kindled intrigue, embroiling the nobility in periodic power struggles. Huayna Capac's death pitted the *panaca* of Atawalpa against that of his brother, Huascar. The ensuing civil war rocked the foundations of Tawantinsuyu's carefully orchestrated social, political and economic institutions. Many of the conquered ethnic lords, who had seen their power usurped by the lords of Cuzco, rebelled. Finally, another more insidious evil dealt the death knell to an already beleaguered Andean people. European diseases such as smallpox and measles, to which indigenous peoples had no natural immunities, had begun making their way down South America shortly after Christopher Columbus's landfall in the Caribbean in 1492. Pizarro did not find an empire in its prime, but one on the verge of collapse.

Yet despite the centuries of political and social upheaval that followed Pizarro's landfall on the beaches of northern Peru, some Andean traditions have survived. Almost five hundred years later we found the secrets of Inca engineering and technology etched on their great monuments of stone, encoded in the village weavings and instilled in the rebuilding of a suspension bridge across the Apurimac.

BIBLIOGRAPHY

STONEHENGE

Atkinson, R.J.C., *Stonehenge* (Penguin Books, London, 1991).

Chippendale, Christopher, *Stonehenge Complete* (Thames & Hudson, London, 1983).

O'Kelly, Michael, *Newgrange: Archaeology, Art and Legend* (Thames & Hudson, London, 1988).

Richard, Julian, *English Heritage, Stonehenge* (Batsford, London, 1991).

Thorpe, Richard, et al., *The Geological Sources and Transport of the Bluestones of Stonehenge, Wiltshire, UK* (Proceedings of the Prehistoric Society 17, part 2, pp. 103–15).

THE PYRAMID

Arnold, Dieter, *Building in Egypt: Pharaonic Stone Masonry* (Oxford University Press, Oxford, 1991).

Clarke, S. and R. Engelbach, *Ancient Egyptian Construction and Architecture* (Dover, New York, 1990). Unabridged copy of original 1930 Ancient Egyptian Building Craft.

Edwards, I.E.S., *The Pyramids of Egypt* (Penguin, London, 1991).

Isler, Martin, 'On Pyramid Building', *The Journal of the American Research Center in Egypt*, 22 (pp. 129–42).

Isler, Martin, 'On Pyramid Building', *The Journal of the American Research Center in Egypt*, 24 (pp. 95–112).

Isler, Martin, 'An Ancient Method of Finding and Extending Direction', *The Journal of the American Research Center in Egypt*, 26 (pp. 191–206).

Lehner, Mark, 'Some observations of the Layout of the Khufu and Khafre Pyramids', *The Journal of the American Research Centre in Egypt*, 20 (pp. 7–25).

McCauley, David, *Pyramid* (Houghton Mifflin, Boston, 1975).

Petrie, W.M.F. and Zahi Hawass, *The Pyramids and Temples of Giseh* (Histories and Mysteries of Man, London, 1990). Reprint with 'Update' by Zahi Hawass.

THE OBELISK

Dibner, Bern, *Moving the Obelisks* (MIT Press, Cambridge, Mass., 1970).

Engelbach, Reginald, *The Problem of the Obelisks* (George H. Doran, New York, 1923).

Habachi, Labib, *The Obelisks of Egypt: Skyscrapers of the Past* (American University in Cairo Press, Cairo, 1984).

THE COLOSSEUM

Cunliffe, Barry, *Rome and her Empire* (Bodley Head, London, 1978).

Graefe, Rainer, *Vela Erunt* (Phillipp von Zabern, Hainz um Rhein, 1979).

Pearson, John, *Arena: The Story of the Colosseum* (Thames & Hudson, London, 1973).

Wiedemann, Thomas, *Emperors and Gladiators* (Routledge, London, 1992).

THE INCAS

Cieza de León, Pedro de, *The Incas* [1553], trans. Harriet de Onis (University of Oklahoma Press, Norman, 1959).

Cobo, Bernabé, *History of the Inca Empire* [1653], trans. Roland Hamilton (University of Texas Press, Austin, 1983).

Cobo, Bernabé, *Inca Religion and Customs* [1653], trans. Roland Hamilton (University of Texas Press, Austin, 1990).

Franquemont, Edward, 'The Bridge at Huinchiri: A Span Across Culture, Technology and Time', Paper presented at the Annual Meeting of the Institute of Andean Studies, Berkeley, California, 7 January 1995.

Garcilaso de la Vega, El Inca, *Royal Commentaries of the Incas and General History of Peru* [1604], *Part I*, trans. Harold V. Livermore (University of Texas Press, Austin, 1966).

Hemming, John, *The Conquest of the Incas* (Penguin Books, Harmondsworth, 1983).

Hyslop, John, *The Inka Road System* (Academic Press Inc., Orlando, 1984).

Hyslop, John, *Inka Settlement Planning* (University of Texas Press, Austin, 1990).

Lee, Vincent R., *The Building of Sacsayhuaman* (Privately published, Wilson, Wyoming, 1987).

Protzen, Jean-Pierre, 'Inca Quarrying and Stonecutting', *Journal of the Society of Architectural Historians*, Vol. XLIV, No. 3, 1985 (pp. 161–82).

Protzen, Jean-Pierre, *Inca Architecture and Construction at Ollantaytambo* (Oxford University Press, New York, 1993).

INDEX